Raising Him Alone

Things Black Women Can Do To Raise Boys To Be Men

David Miller, M.Ed.
and Matthew Stevens

For information regarding lectures, workshops, seminars or products designed by the authors please visit us online at

David Miller
Urban Leadership Institute
www.urbanyouth.org

&

Matthew Stevens
www.EmpowerTodaysYouth.com

For more information on the Raising Him Alone Campaign visit **www.raisinghimalone.com**

ISBN # 9780965902823
Copyright 2009

All Rights Reserved

No part of this book may be reproduced in any form
without written permission from the publisher.

Book cover:
Book layout: Natalie | www.steelorchid.com

> There are many challenges that single mom's raising African-American males face. One of the biggest is the educational system. In many instances, black boys are quickly diagnosed with Attention Deficit Disorder or presumptuously tracked as special needs when the issue is not necessarily special needs but diverse strengths and learning styles. Boys tend to develop their gross motor skills before their fine motor skills, but the traditional education system is not designed to nurture these strengths. This poses a challenge for mothers who have children that are misdiagnosed and are placed in educational environments that work from a deficit model rather than a strengths-based one.

Cassandra Mack, MSW, author of "The Black Man's Little Book of Encouragement" and "Single Mother's Little Book of Wisdom"

> To break negative cycles in our communities, we must build from the foundation up, starting with our families. An African American boy's primary parent is most often his mother. How a mama raises her son can change generations. I applaud Raising Him Alone (book) and the Raising Him Alone Campaign for recognizing this truth and acting on it.

Ms. Kelly, founder, singlemamahood.com

> Raising my two sons was difficult but I had an extended family that supported me all the way. I wish a book like this was around when I was a single mother raising two boys in a tough Brooklyn community.

Sheron "umi" Smith, author, motivational speaker and mother of Mos Def

> The Raising Him Alone Campaign and book are critical to the success of our sons and daughters. The book underscores the values of the village in taking responsibility for ensuring the spiritual and emotional well being of our sons. We are losing our men and the campaign reminds us that we are the ones we have been waiting for.

**Dr. Brenda Greene, Brooklyn, New York
Mother of rapper Talib Kewli**

> Raising him alone can be difficult, if you are alone, but remember you are not. You now have a network of support. Just reach out and someone will be there to catch you.

**Dr. Mahalia Hines, Chicago, Illinois
Mother of rapper/actor Common**

My husband recently passed away and our son is so angry. The Raising Him Alone Campaign and book has helped us secure family counseling.

**Brenda Muhammad
Newark, NJ**

I am 72 years old and raising six male grand children. This book provides practical advice that helps me deal with these boys"

**Emma Johnson
South Hill, Virgina**

I am glad that someone has written a book on raising boys. My son has ADHD and I am not sure where to turn for help. Being a single mother raising a boy with challenges can be overwhelming.

**Gina Jones
Los Angeles, California**

I am raising three boys alone. No father, no uncles or other male role models in my sons lives. This book has helped me realize that I must create a village of men to surround my son.

**Davina Joseph
Baltimore, MD**

To all of the mothers far and wide who asked us to write this book.

ACKNOWLEDGEMENTS

This book is dedicated to millions of single mothers who struggle daily with the challenges of raising healthy and productive boys to become responsible men. The project has been part of our collective vision for several years. Working day in and day out trying to develop initiatives designed to improve the life chances of Black males, we came to the conclusion that greater energy and resources needed to focus on empowering single mothers. These single mothers are often isolated and marginalized.

Although painful, the endless statistics about Black male development tell us that we must focus on positive parenting strategies. That is if we are serious about reducing the likelihood that young Black males will become gang members, drop out of school and become the next generation of young males who will have a baby and walk away.

We are thankful to all of the women who allowed us into their lives to understand the magnitude of raising a boy alone in a toxic society. The hours of one-on-one telephone conversations and focus groups interviews have been a valuable addition to this book.

A special thanks goes to mothers in Baltimore, MD., and Newark, N.J., who provided a great deal of insight and information to launch the Raising Him Alone Campaign.

David would like to thank Kristance Coates, Anisa Harrington-Crawford, Regina Salliey, Dink, Catrice Alphonso, Dana Bankins, Stacie Price, Kim Armstrong, Darlene Brown, Darlene Walker, Pastor Linwood & Karen Bethea, my wife Dr. Karla Paylor and children.

Special thanks to Bettye Blaize for all your to support the vision of the Urban Leadership Institute. Your commitment has been invaluable.

Matt would like thank all of the single mothers on his street who raised him and his friends: Ms. Stevens (Matt and Corey), Ms. Keith (Sean, Tommy and Rocky), Ms. Lee (Robert), Ms. Kinney (Mike), Ms. Hall (Mark), Ms. Dale (Scott and Jessie), Ms. Davis (Quincy and Duquan), Ms. Freeman (Tony), Ms. Byrd (Kyle), Ms. Townsend (DT), Ms. Waller (Jay, Joe, Hoppie, George, Hassan, Chris, and Kenny), my wife Gina Stevens and children.

Many heart felt thanks to:

Laurie Willis, editor, for your keen eye, patience and support.

Lee McDonald & Charlotte Reid (Renaissance Public Relations) for your encouragement, support, wisdom and knowledge.

LaMarr Shields, Kevin Powell, Patrick Oliver, Kenneth Braswell, Joel Austin, Richard Rowe, Ademola Ekulona and Adeyemi Bandele for your expertise in the areas of male development and reconnecting fathers to their families.

We hope that Raising Him Alone will serve as a resource for single mothers who are committed to ensuring that their sons grow to become strong men/husbands and fathers. Raising Him Alone is a guide that supports mothers in developing a blueprint to help their sons complete high school, avoid drugs and alcohol, and steer clear of prisons and jails.

We hope that Raising Him Alone compels mothers to band together to address the challenges of being a single mother. After reading please make sure you pass this book along to other mothers who can benefit from lessons learned and the wisdom of others who have successfully navigated the world of being a single parent.

Thanks to Sheron "umi" Smith (Mos Def's Mom), Dr. Mahalia Hines (Common's Mom) and Dr. Brenda Greene (Talib Kweli's Mom) for being exceptional mothers. Thanks for helping us launch the Raising Him Alone Campaign.

Special thanks to the vision of the Open Society Institute for creating a movement among foundations to support positive Black male development. Thanks to Shawn Dove for you leadership with the Open Society Institute's Campaign for Black Male Achievement.

Finally, after reading Raising Him Alone we hope that you will visit our Raising Him Alone website at www.raisinghimalone.com. The website was designed to provide ongoing support and advocacy for single mothers. As you navigate the website you find several tools designed to connect single mothers with advice, reading materials and strategies to support healthy male development. The site features sections that address a number of challenges single mothers face. Each is broken up into simple recommendations that can easily be applied. Below is a list of these critical areas:

- :: **Basic Rules for Single Mothers**
- :: **Reconnecting Fathers**
- :: **Quick Tips for Single Mothers Raising Boys**
- :: **Tips for Single Mothers Raising Teenage Boys**
- :: **Single Mothers Raising a Son with a Disability/Navigating the Special Education system**
- :: **Grandmothers Raising Boys**
- :: **Dating Rules for Single Mothers**

Other sections of the site provide advice and suggestions on how to talk to their sons about sensitive issues such as sex, drugs and staying in schools.

Contents

Introduction

How to Use This Book

Chapter 1: There Is No Place Like Home
:: Expect Him To Be a Man
:: Monitor How He Spends His Time
:: Protect His Emotional & Spiritual Life
:: Help Him Develop His Voice
:: Define Self-Esteem With Him
:: Surround Him With Positive Men(tors)
:: Financial Literacy
:: Search His Room
:: Keep Him Safe on the Internet
:: Meet the Parents (of His Friends)

Chapter 2: School House Blues
:: Meet His Teacher
:: Start a Family Reading Club
:: Teach African History
:: Just Say No To Special Ed
:: Teach Him Another Language

Chapter 3: Navigating the Hood
:: Teach Him How to Defend Himself
:: Teach Him How to Treat a Lady
:: Keep Him Out of the Criminal Justice System
:: 10 Rules of Survival If Stopped by the Police
:: He Is Arrested
:: Keep Him Out of a Gang
:: Select the Right Coach

Chapter 4: Protecting the King (Health Wellness)
:: Expect Him to Take Care of Himself
:: Keep Him Smiling (Dentists)
:: Let's Talk About Sex
:: Should He Get the Tattoo?

Chapter 5: Reconnecting Dad
:: Fatherlessness on Boys
:: Blame Yourself (Blame Game)
:: When Dad Wants to Come Back
:: Tell Him He Is the Man of the House
:: Village Dads

Chapter 6: Amazing Grandparents
:: Grandparents Raising Boys: The New Generation of Amazing Grandparents

Chapter 7: Final Thoughts

INTRODUCTION

Black women love their sons and raise their daughters

So many things have changed for women in the new millennium. One thing that remains the same is a woman's commitment to her children and doing the very best job in raising them. As an academic counselor that specializes in counseling adolescent male students, I come in contact with single mothers that are raising boys on a daily basis. All of them desire to raise their sons to be fathers, husbands and respectable men in the community. Quite often I am asked for advice by women who are looking for things they can do to raise their sons to be men. This is the reason we wrote this book.

A common phrase used in the African American community is: "Black women love their sons and raise their daughters." I first heard this quote used by Dr. Jawanza Kunjufu, author of Conspiracy to Destroy Black Boys.

Dr. Kunjufu used this statement in the context of helping women design strategies to combat the conspiracy he asserted was taking place in the destruction of their male children.

Raising Him Alone

He made a point to clearly indicate his intention was not to blame Black women for the condition of their sons. Conversely, this statement, in addition to his life's work, was geared to acknowledging some of the differences found in the process of child rearing between men and women. In my opinion, Black woman have done a phenomenal job in keeping the Black community afloat. As a product of a single-parent household headed by my mother, I can attest to the hard work that it takes to raise a son in this society.

This book follows Dr. Kunjufu's lead, and it is designed as a tool to help mothers raising boys. It provides a number of practical, proven, and easy to implement strategies that help avoid some of the social pitfalls many of our sons encounter that prevent them from achieving their fullest potential.

Finally, the election of Barak Obama, the 44th president of the United States and the first African American one, moves to the forefront the role single mothers play in producing healthy and responsible African American males. Obama the product of multiracial parenting was raised by his mother and grandmother. This is significant as we grapple with the role of men/fathers in raising the next generation of Black males in our communities. The parenting provided by the matriarchs in the Obama family provide glaring evidence that women can help boys become healthy and responsible men.

This is a time in American history when so many communities suffer from the loss of sober, responsible, spiritually guided African American males to step up in the lives of boys as fathers and role models. The statistics are often daunting. For example, the most recent report on graduation rates among African American males published by the Schott Foundation indicates that in many U.S. cities

African American males are dropping out at rates that exceed 65 percent. The cities include but are not limited to Indianapolis, Detroit and Baltimore. With Indianapolis having the lowest graduation rates in the nation among African American males. Indianapolis and Detroit's graduation rates among African American males can only be viewed as a public health concern. With 19 percent and 20 percent, respectively, these rates should be the focus of every major conversation related to child well being, community development, incarceration and family development.

Like many issues within the African American community, however, these statistics seldom make the box scores. While people in Detroit were preoccupied with 0-16 record posted by the Detroit Lions thousands of Black boys in the city of Detroit are failing.

To this end it is our hope that Raising Him Alone will sound the alarm that boys of African descent, now more than ever need the support, love and guidance from their families and community to survive and thrive within a toxic society.

Raising Him Alone is part of a larger campaign to reclaim our sons and encourage our men and fathers to come back home to support the raising of strong Black boys who eventually will become men. Men like Barak Obama, Geoffrey Canada, Randall Pickett, Sidney Portier, Paul Robeson, Langston Hughes and Eddie Brown.

These men, along with a host of other Black men, have set the standard of excellence in our community. If we truly want the best for our sons, we must love, appreciate and support the mothers in the lives of our sons.

How to use this book

This book is a one-stop shop for single mothers tasked with raising a male child in a toxic society. While we realize that raising a male child can be difficult, millions of women struggle and toil year end and year old to provide their sons with the love and guidance needed to become successful. Raising Him Alone is a cutting-edge resource that deals with increased awareness of the role of mothers in raising boys to become men, as well as assisting mothers in developing a life plan for their son. The book is written based on interviews with single mothers who have raised boys to become successful men and interviews with mothers who are currently raising boys. These interviews included a cross section of mothers from across the United States. Many of these mothers have raised sons who have attended elite colleges and universities, such as Morehouse, Howard, Hampton, Harvard, Princeton, and Yale. They are mothers who have raised sons who are fortunate to have been drafted into the NFL and NBA. Other mothers struggled to keep their sons alive, to see them graduate from high school, enter the work force, get married and start a family.

This book is written as a source of hope and inspiration for mothers who at times felt alone and unable to cope. We hope that like many other books on your night stand that you will refer to it when you have no one else to call and you need some sound advice.

We all know that we live in a society that promotes quick fixes. Raising Him Alone is not a quick fix, but rather a book that attempts to make sense out things that will affect you and your son. Things like understanding new trends, technology and fashion.

Parents in today's society are confronted with hip-hop/rap music, a genre of music that often portrays young Black males as gangsters and drug dealers. Text messaging, Facebook and Myspace have become the new vehicles for youth to communicate.

While we are excited about young Black males increasing access to technology, we are concerned about exposure to inappropriate material.
Our sons are inundated with a variety of negative messages that promote narrow definitions manhood and masculinity. Many of these messages are shaped by Hollywood's exploitative movies and videos aired on MTV, BET and VH1. Far too often these messages promote irresponsible sexual activity, gang membership and a culture of violence.

At the end of the day we believe parents have unlimited power to monitor what their sons listen to and view on television. Whether its periodic IPod checks, developing a television viewing schedule and monitoring cell phones, parents have the ability to determine levels what they will allow their sons to watch and listen to.

Raising Him Alone will encourage you to strive to be a better mother and understand the power of proactive parenting. Raising Him Alone proves that single mothers can successfully raise a healthy and productive male child. Enjoy growing up with your son.

CHAPTER 1
There Is No Place Like Home

> God surely knew what he was doing when he set up the arrangement of having two parents rear a child. It's extremely hard raising my son alone because my son craves male attention.
>
> ***Single mother of two sons, Washington, D.C.***

THERE'S NO PLACE LIKE HOME

How do Black women raise boys to be men? A number of troubling statistics seem to state that there may not be an answer to this question. This is a question that we are constantly asked during book signings, public appearances and radio interviews. Often this question dominates any discussion on the African American community in which we participate. This question usually is coupled with a few examples by women who are passionate about raising their sons but realize the numerous challenges head.

Recently, while speaking at a church in rural Georgia, a very distinguished African American mother in her mid 40s discussed her dilemma.

In short the mom recently received her M.B.A. from Georgia Tech University. She was employed by a large corporation outside of Atlanta. As she continued to share, it became apparent that the mom like so many we talk to on a regular basis was crying for help. Despite having an M.B.A. and a six-figure income, she is part of a club that is often misunderstood and mislabeled. The mom and her son were part of the "Absent Daddy Club." The mom met a young man during college. He said all the right things, he was an engineer major and he was in a fraternity on campus. He was on the dean's list, and he had interned at one of the top electrical engineering firms in Atlanta.

Raising Him Alone

He was in his last year on his way to grad school, and she was completing her sophomore year. She got pregnant, and the rest is history. The product of this union is Kevin, an extremely bright 10-year-old African American male child growing up without a father.

According to Schott Foundation Report- Public Education and Black Male Students (2005) and Why We Can't Wait: A Case for Philanthropic Action. Opportunities for Improving the Life Outcomes of African American Males (2007), young Black males in America are dropping out of high school at an alarming rate, are dying at an alarming rate, and are more likely to be involved in the juvenile justice system than to matriculate to college. All of these statistics contribute to higher rates of under- and unemployment, diminished emotional and financial wellbeing among men of color.

According to Schott Foundation Report- Public Education and Black Male Students (2005) and Why We Can't Wait: A Case for Philanthropic Action. Opportunities for Improving the Life Outcomes of African American Males (2007), young Black males in America are dropping out of high school at an alarming rate, are dying at an alarming rate, and are more likely to be involved in the juvenile justice system than to matriculate to college. All of these statistics contribute to higher rates of under- and unemployment, diminished emotional and financial well being among men of color.

| *Raising Him Alone*

:: *Setting High Expectations for Him*
:: *Monitoring How He Spends His Time*
:: *Defining Self-Esteem With Him*
:: *Surrounding Him With Positive Men(tors)*
:: *Practicing Financial Literacy*
:: *Meeting the Parents (His Friends)*
:: *Designing an Exit Strategy (for Him)*

Setting High Expectations of Him

If you can control a man's thinking, you do not have to worry about his actions.
Carter G. Woodson

An examination of African American history provides insight on how low expectations of Black men have shaped their current situation. In *The Post Traumatic Slave Syndrome*, Dr. Joy Leary explores how slavery impacted and continues to impact how black men behave based on low expectations set by slave masters and their families.

According to Leary, slave masters maintained low expectations of Black men to assert control over them. She points to *The Willie Lynch Letter: The Making of a Slave* as one example of how and why low expectations were held for black men. The author of the letter asserted *"taking control of the Nigger's mind" as an essential part of making him obedient."* This letter was allegedly shared with slave holders across the country and became the "Slave's Owner Manual." Slave owners used low expectations of Black men to control their minds and consequently ensured their continued servitude.
In **The Mis-Education of the Negro**, Carter G. Woodson states:

Raising Him Alone

When you control a man's thinking you do not have to worry about his actions. You do not have to tell him not to stand here or go yonder. He will find his "proper place" and will stay in it. You do not need to send him to the back door. He will go without being told. In fact, if there is no back door, he will cut one for his special benefit. His education makes it necessary."

Leary explores the role Black women played in setting and maintaining low expectations of male children. She asserts that this practice was a structured method of protecting Black boys and was seen as a survival mechanism.

During slavery Black males that exhibited behaviors consistent with manhood were murdered in the most egregious manners. Witnessing these crimes and as a part of their socialization, Black women were encouraged to raise their sons to be boys rather than men to ensure their survival. Dr. Joy Leary and others (Carter G. Woodson, Na'im Akbar, Manning Marble, Lenwood Gunther) argue that these mentalities subconsciously have been passed on from generation to generation. They say that some of these protective measures unknowingly are practiced by today's Black mothers.

> *The process of Black manhood must be defined as being irreversible.*
> **Na'im Akbar**

HOW CAN MOTHERS RAISE EXPECTATIONS OF OUR SONS?

Our first suggestion is to define manhood as a process that is irreversible. By irreversible we mean that once a boy becomes a man there are certain things that can no longer be acceptable. A passage in the Bible states:

> "When I became a MAN",
> I put away childish things."
> I CORINTHIANS 13:11

Young men must first be taught to see themselves as being involved in a process that is natural and expected. This process for a woman is defined clearly by society and biology when she starts her menstrual cycle.

During this process a girl is often told that she is "no longer a little girl." After this "talk," the mother or a caring woman in the family helps the girl understand the process as it relates to her directly and indirectly. The young woman is notified that she must now do certain things to take care of herself. In addition, she is prepared for the mental and emotional factors that are associated with this process.

Unlike his female counterpart, males do not have as clear of a social process that draws the line in the sand as it relates to leaving boyish things behind. In certain cultures a rites of passage is mandated by the village where all males participate in a series of learning exercises that provide clear expectations of manhood. In Roots (1975) Alex Hailey described this process as it relates to Africans. Hailey portrayed the African rites of passage by showing Kunta Kenta and his contemporaries leaving their village as boys and returning as men. During their process they were taught how to be men. Upon his return Kunta discussed with his mother his new position and her, his family's and community's higher expectations of him.

Raising Him Alone

Somehow we must return to the rites of passage for our boys if we expect them to understand and succeed in their role as men.

One of the first strategies we suggest is telling our boys that the process of manhood is irreversible. In Natural Psychology and Human Transformation, Na'im Akbar compares the process of adolescence, as it relates to young men, with that of a caterpillar. First, he points to similar characteristics of a baby and a caterpillar (totally dependent on someone else). Second, he describes similar characteristics as they go into adolescence (increasing independence). Last, he highlights the distinctions of a caterpillar and a boy once they complete adolescence. Here Akbar notes that unlike the caterpillar, which is now a butterfly, the boy has the opportunity to live up to expectations and become a man or he can revert back to boyish things.

THE PROCESS OF MANHOOD

Infant	Adolescence	Adult

We urge mothers to ensure that this process is complete and irreversible by mandating that their sons let go of boyish ways as they become adolescents, and particularly as they become young men. This can occur in a number of ways, which we explore throughout the book. To end this chapter we would like to explore a way to start this process, which is by reading more books and playing less video games.

On average most American boys between the ages of 8-16 have ten times more video games than books on their shelves. While there is nothing wrong with teenage boys playing video games, recent reports indicate that the games are becoming more of a distraction than any game should be in a child's life. Dr. Lenard Sax author of Boys Adrift argues that video games are having a profound impact on the academic and social lives of boys. Parents should decide how much, how often their sons will be able to play video games. Parents must create limits and boundaries related to video game usage.

Other strategies to manage this concern are designing strategies that use video games as an incentive. For example a books-read-to-video-games–played ratio. Each parent must determine what is best for her son, but on average a boy should read two books for every video game he owns.

QUESTIONS FOR PARENTS

1. How many video games does your son own?

2. How many books has your son read this month?

3. How often have you and your son visited the library this year? Do either one of you have a local library card?

MONITOR HOW HE SPENDS HIS TIME

Malcolm X once said, "Time is the one thing which can manage you if you fail to manage it." He made this statement to Alex Hailey during the writing of his autobiography. Malcolm had disdain for men who did not wear a watch because it was a clear indication of his failure to manage his own time, according to Hailey. The man had to continue to ask someone else, "What time is it?"

DOES YOUR SON HAVE HIS OWN WATCH?

Use Table on the following page to outline your son's daily activities on a school day.

TIME MANAGEMENT SCHEDULE

Time	Activity
3:00	
4:00	
5:00	
6:00	
7:00	
8:00	
9:00	
10:00	
11:00	

Raising Him Alone

PROTECT HIS EMOTIONAL & SPIRITUAL LIFE

Growing up is always a complex phase for youth of any age, any race and socioeconomic background. When we examine the plethora of challenges (underachievement, homicide and incarceration) that impact Black male youth, however, parents should be prepared to consider the emotional and spiritual essence of Black males.

Any parent who has successfully raised a Black male child in America has struggled to understand and interpret his feelings and emotions. Often during conversation parents find it difficult to ask questions regarding feelings and emotions related to an event that has occurred in school, community or at home.

As our sons navigate the world, they learn early that demonstrating feelings and emotions can be a slippery slop in the male world. From sadness to frustration to joy and love Black males like other males share the range of human emotions. Without the right training and support, however, many young Black males grow up believing many of the stereotypical images of Black manhood and masculinity presented on BET, MTV and VH1. These images -- coupled with Hollywood's ongoing portrayal of the Black male as dangerous, misguided and out of control -- have created a self-fulfilling prophecy among countless Black males.

No cell phone, no video game or designer pair of tennis shoes will ever teach young Black males fundamental lessons of courage, empathy, compassion and love. These are traits that we are supposed to learn from our parents at an early age.

Like many of my colleagues for the last 15 years, I have struggled to respond to the pleas of parents searching for ways to get their sons to "open up!" Usually the parents say their sons provide them with vague responses and one-word statements. These statements range from, "I am cool" to "Everything is good." As one parent put it: "My son's father passed away in September of 2005. Leading up to the funeral I expected my son to say something about his father even though they did not have a good relationship. Two years latter my son asked me, while at the dinner table, "Do you think daddy ever loved us?"

Over the years I have had so many conversations with parents about cultivating and protecting the emotional life of boys. While many parents realize the importance of understanding the emotional intelligence of their sons, the issue of spirituality and Black males in seldom addressed. The issue of religion within the Black community always has been a "hot button" topic.

Key Tips for Parents
(Rescuing the Emotional Lives of Our Boys)

DON'T BLAME HIM FOR YOUR MISTAKES

Mom let's face it you are mad because of mistakes you made. It's not his fault (your son) that you got pregnant. So why are you so angry? Does your son remind you of the man you would like to forget? Your pain will destroy your relationship with your son as well as point him down a road full of destruction.

ADMIT WHEN YOU ARE WRONG

Parenting a Black male child can be difficult but to the degree you can strengthen your relationship will provide him with a core set of values and beliefs. The relationship, however, cannot be one-sided. Often we are wrong as parents and find it difficult to apologize and admit when we are at fault. Admitting when we are wrong can help our sons develop a healthy emotional and spiritual foundation. If you are your son's first teacher, you have the power to teach him some very powerful lessons that he will remember for the rest of his life.

AVOID ARGUING/NEVER PART WITHOUT SOME LEVEL OF RECONCILIATION

We get calls consistently from parents who battle with their sons regularly. The question we always ask is why argue. It takes at least two people to become involved in an argument. Although we realize that conflicts and arguments can be healthy, at what point do you realize that consistently arguing with your son is not working.

Additionally, we know based on statistics from the Centers for Disease Control and Prevention as well as watching any news broadcast in America that arguments are responsible for an overwhelming number of murders. For African American boys and men, homicide has become one of the leading causes of death.

We recommend setting boundaries with your sons in dealing with issues that may lead to an argument. We believe developing a system will bring more peace and respect to your home.

Life is too precious to stay mad at your son. Try to find common ground to begin the healing process.

LISTEN
(Mom listen twice as much as you talk)

Allow your son an opportunity to talk, regardless of how mad or difficult the conversation may be. Always remember you were a child/teen at one time in your life. How did it feel when you thought your parents wouldn't listen to you?

Your son will appreciate the opportunity to talk, and you will begin to notice how willing he is to discuss areas of concerns. This process will not materialize overnight. It will take some time.

** Parents please review the 10 Non-Negotiable Laws of Parenting Him Alone

10 Non-Negotiable Laws of Parenting Him Alone

1. **Sacrifice** - Raising healthy & productive children will require difficult decisions. Just because his daddy "rolled out" buying your the son the world will not help with the healing process.

2. **Family Planning** - Create a plan for the family. Create a financial, academic and spiritual plan. Too many African American males are being raised without a "blueprint" for the future.

3. **Respect, Honor & Pride** - Instill a sense of pride for the family. A child should never disgrace the family name.

4. **Limits** - Set boundaries for our sons. Effective single parenting begins with setting up clear systems of accountability. Activities such as curfew, television consumption, and video game usage must be strongly enforced.

5. **Desire** - Want your children to have a better life than you have ...

6. **Wisdom** - Today's parent has to be smarter than ever before. What kind of music does your child listen to? What's in your child's room?

7. **Firm & Flexible** – Serving as the disciplinarian in the home is important. Make sure that you are not afraid to discipline your child.

8. **Listen** - Now more than ever we need to be willing to listen to our children. Even if we don't like the conversation, our sons must be willing to share feelings and emotions regarding dating, sex and other peer-related influences.

9. **Explain your decisions** - Let your children know what you expect. When they do not meet the expectations be ready to explain your concerns.

10. **Stay involved** - Know all aspects of your child's life (friends, hang outs, strengths & challenges). Don't be afraid to search your son's room and/or search his belongings. These things can help you save your son's life.

| Raising Him Alone

HELP YOUNG BLACK MALES DEVELOP THEIR VOICE

In the early 1990s Carol Gillian from Harvard University introduced a body of literature on "helping girls find their voice." This work focused heavily on helping girls understanding their essence as well as developing the ability to communicate and be assertive in a society that often minimizes girls and women.

In general, boys have problems communicating and talking about their shortcomings, which historically have been viewed as non-masculine activities. The voices of so many young African American males are stifled by Hollywood's psychic assault on the Black male image. Whether it's musical artists such as 50 Cent, Souljah Boy or Snoop Dog, the endless portrayals of Black males as thugs, pimps and gangsters must be challenged by parents.

At the 78th Academy Awards "It's Hard Out Here for a Pimp" a song written by hip-hop group Three 6 Mafia and Cedric Coleman for the film Hustle & Flow won Best Original Song. The song was performed in the film by veteran African American actor Terrence Howard and newly rising Hollywood star Taraji P. Henson. These portrayals of Black males undermine the cultural values we need to promote among young males and the community.

As long as we allow rap videos, professional athletes and drug dealers to shape images of manhood and masculinity, we will continue to produce young Black males who are ill-equipped to accept the mantel of manhood.

| *Raising Him Alone*

The following are a few recommendations for mothers to help encourage their son to find his voice. Many of these recommendations are probably things that you already know. The little things, however, tend to get pushed to the side when we think about paying bills, checking homework and the other daily tasks on which parents are focused.

EXPOSE TO THE ARTS

Makes our sons more well rounded individuals and provides them with an understanding of culture. Immersing your son in activities that promote art and culture allow a greater understanding of humanity. Dance, music and art (painting, sculptures and visual mediums) are key pillars within society.

GET TO KNOW YOUR SON

Often by the time boys get to high school many parents realize that they do not know their son. As a parent of a male child knowing all aspects of your son's life is critical. Developing this kind of relationship will require a great deal of time focused on talking with and listening to your son.

CREATE FUN TIME

No matter how old your son gets it is rewarding for mothers and sons to spend time together. Whether it's going to the mall, playing video games or playing catch, mothers can be active in aspects of their sons life.

IDENTIFY HIS SELF ESTEEM

Does you son have high or low self-esteem? Self-esteem is defined as the way people feel about themselves in a particular area based on past performance. According to this definition, people may have high and low self-esteem simultaneously. It is essential that Black boys understand how to identify their levels of self-esteem and the following

KS2 + A = SE

This is actually an acronym that stands for Knowledge of Self-Image and Skills (KS2) plus Accomplishments (A) equal Self-Esteem (SE). Used properly, this outline can help a mother initiate a number of conversations with her son. Conversations should help boys to recognize what they do well and where they may need improvements. Suggested use of the outline includes:

1. Consider an area in life where you are considered an expert. (Example: I am a good public speaker.)

2. Identify a skill(s) you have in that area (Example: I am able to speak to a large group of people and maintain their interest in a variety of topics.)

3. List one or more accomplishments you have obtained in that area (Example: For two years in a row, I was selected to be the keynote speaker at an international conference.)

In this case I identified my self-esteem as high in the area of public speaking. It is suggested to always discover where a person's self esteem is high before discovering where it requires improvements. This helps recognize unique qualities. In my case I realized that I am a good public speaker because I work hard every day to improve.

Once a boy feels good about himself, it becomes easier for him to recognize where he may need improvements and provides an incentive for action. My self-esteem is low in the area of basketball. The same thing can and should be done in other areas.

HOW TO IDENTIFY LOW SELF ESTEEM

1. I am not athletically inclined and particularly not in basketball. (Self-image)

2. I am slow, uncoordinated and a bit overweight. Also I cannot dribble or shoot the basketball well. (Skills)

3. Every time I go on the basketball court for a pick-up game, I never get selected as a team member. (Accomplishments)

My two options are to do something to improve in this area or to accept the fact that I am not good at basketball. The latter has the potential to negatively affect other parts of my life. By accepting the fact that I am not good at basketball, I could continue to go out on the court and perform below average or I could give up.

Performing below average almost guarantees that I will not get selected to play by other players, and giving up eliminates a good source of exercise. Therefore, I need to practice in order to prevent slipping into physical and psychological mediocrity. Significant numbers of young men that I work with have low self-esteem in academic areas such as math and science. If they are allowed to simply state, "I am not good at math" or "Science has always been my worst subject" or God forbid "Doing well in math and science is acting white," we severely hamper their potential for future opportunities.

WHERE IS YOUR SONS SELF–ESTEEM: HIGH AND LOW?

Completing this grid will help you define self-esteem with your son. It is suggested that you perform this activity during when you have at least one hour.

1. Discuss and select an area where your son has high and low self-esteem. Starting with his high self-esteem and stroking his ego, ask him where he thinks he is "The Man." Do the same thing for areas he feels he needs to make improvements. (Self-image)

2. Identify three skills that support his assertions.

3. List three accomplishments or failures (lack of accomplishments) that support his assertions

5. Design a time-based Improvement plan for improving self-esteem in each area.

My self-esteem was high in the area of public speaking, but I know that I want to become a better speaker. Therefore, I will take an advanced public speaking course at a community college. My goal is to master the ability to speak at news conferences. On the other hand, my self-esteem is low about playing basketball; therefore, I plan to join a gym and work out consistently on my lower body strength and cardiovascular activities. In one semester I should see results in both areas.

Raising Him Alone

SELF-ESTEEM GRID

High Self-Esteem	
Self-image	
Skills	
Accomplishment	
Improvement Plan	
Low Self-Esteem	
Self-image	
Skills	
Accomplishment	
Improvement Plan	

SURROUND HIM WITH POSITIVE MEN(TORS)

Finding responsible, sober and spiritually guided men to serve as role models for our sons is something that we consistently discuss when we speak to parent groups, to churches and civic groups.

> I do not expect the white media to create positive black male images.
> **Huey P. Newton**

Teaching our boys about boyhood and manhood is essential if we expect them to become responsible men/husbands and fathers. This process of teaching a boy to become a man is an ancient principle that pre-dates the formation of the United States. In most traditional cultures, a formal process or "rite of passage," served as the gold standard for determining manhood.

This process usually included a series of development, analytical, spiritual and physical tests in which the boys participated under the direction of a "council of elders." This council was usually composed of the most respected men in the village.

Many have written extensively about the rite of passage process and its practical application in addressing many of the historical, cultural and environmental challenges that confront boys of African descent. Today many community-based groups across the United States and abroad offer "African-centered rites of passage" programs to support positive male development using a cultural framework.

In an earlier section of the book, I outlined Na'im Akbar's theory that states manhood is an irreversible process. Akbar, and other scholars like him, has provided the intellectual foundation for defining manhood. Mentors actually put this theory into practice by teaching boys how to be men.

Mentors can be found in a number of places. If a mother asks an individual man to mentor her son, she must understand the role of mentoring. While mentoring has been proven effective, the challenges is recruiting African American male mentors.

In 2008 Miller authored Man Up: Recruiting & Retaining African American Male Mentors. The report added a valuable perspective to the views and perceptions that African American have toward mentoring. Although the project surveyed a small sample of African American men (576) from diverse backgrounds, educational levels and incomes, we believe the study provides some evidence of the limitations of mentoring programs.

This challenge has created a huge vacuum within the mentoring world. With so many programs trying to recruit African American male mentors, a void has been created. This coupled with the oversaturation of mentoring programs has left many mothers searching for reliable mentors.

THE ROLE OF MENTORING

POINT A → **POINT B**

Mentoring is a process that helps a person progress from point A (their current position) to Point B (a desired or improved position.) A number of factors must be understood so that the process and relationship works effectively.

WHAT IS A MENTOR?

A mentor is a friend and guide.

Mentors serve as friends who assist mentees by showing unconditional positive regard. A friend recognizes when the other person is wrong and is able to separate the deed from the person. Working with boys can be a struggle because they tend to be a bit hard-headed and almost never seem to learn things the easy way. When a mentor approaches his relationship as a friendship, he can see beyond immaturity, inexperience and poor decision-making (to name a few things) and provide direction.

Mentors are also guides. As a part of one of his stand-up performances Richard Pryor once said, "There is no such thing as an old fool, because fools don't get old!" Every man on the planet earth can remember what it was like to be a boy and the feelings he had during specific moments. Fundamentally boys and girls have different experiences growing up. From dealing with school bullies to attractions to members of the opposite sex and all things in between. Events such as having a wet dream, shaving, wondering when is a good time to kiss a girl and graduating from high school are areas where boys require guidance from someone who has experienced it.

WHAT A MENTOR IS NOT?

A mentor is not a replacement for fathers.

Mentors should never have the role, responsibility or authority to make decisions as a father. Specifically, mentors should never be allowed to punish children. When something occurs that requires punishment, the mentor should be directed to involve the parent or appropriate authorities. Mentors also should not give money to a child. That includes money for any purpose or the purchase of gifts.

HOW TO SELECT A MENTOR(S)?

Who was your mentor? It is likely that a number of people will come to mind when you think of the person or people who taught or influenced you in certain areas. You could have had a mentor who taught you how to cook, another that influenced your taste in music, and yet another who helped you in math class. The great thing about a mentor is that they can come at any point in a person's life and from any sector of the community.

While some express concerns in matching African American males with mentors that are not African American men, I don't share that opinion. If the goal of a mentor relationship is to teach an African American male teenager how to shave, I see merit in insisting that his mentor be an African American male with a similar skin type. This is done because the mentor can guide the mentee in an area where he has personal experience. When a mother is seeking a mentor to guide her son in the area of Web site design, I would recommend anyone with experience in Web site design.

BEWARE OF THE WOLF!

Before a mother attempts to select a mentor, regardless of their race, ethnicity or occupation it is strongly recommended that a federal criminal record check be conducted to ensure the potential mentor does not have a troubled past. A federal criminal record check can be obtained through the local police department and is different from a local police check. Quite often local police checks do not provide valuable information on crimes that may have been committed outside of the local jurisdiction. The record check is sometimes seen as an extra step and some volunteers may decide not to participate because of the time that it consumes. It, however, is probably the most important part of the mentor process.

Do you have a relative in your family who you know should not be around kids, but other people in the community think is an upstanding citizen? If so, then you are well aware of how a person can appear one way and actually be another way.

The Big Brother and Big Sister of New York and Fordham University Mentor Supervisor Certificate Program use an entire class to discuss how international organizations of men who desire to have sex with boys train their members to maneuver

Raising Him Alone

the mentor screening processes. It is, therefore, strongly recommended that anyone who is selected to serve as a mentor be screened thoroughly.
PLEASE DON'T TRUST ANYONE!

QUESTIONS TO ASK MENTOR REFERENCE

- How long have you known the person?
- In what capacity have you known the person?
- What do you consider the person's weaknesses and strengths?
- Do you know of any reason this person might not be appropriate to work with my child on a one-on-one basis?
- How does the person respond to stressful situations?
- Do you feel this person is in a position to make a one-year commitment to a child?
- Would you feel comfortable having this person volunteer with your child?
- To your knowledge, has the person had any criminal convictions? If so, what are they?
- If you have any additional information you think might be helpful, please comment.

WHERE TO FIND MENTORS?

When possible it is highly recommended to seek mentors through established, trusted and proven mentor programs. Black men are the hardest group to recruit to be mentors. Most black men that work full-time jobs, own their own business and/or other time consuming activities, simply do not have the time to volunteer for one-on-one mentor programs. We, therefore, suggest participating in group mentor programs such as:

Big Brothers and Big Sisters of America is the premier mentor program in the United States. They have a structured program, proven mentor screening and matching policy, and it is the leader in the training of mentor programs. They are located in most U.S. cities, www.bbbs.com

Police Departments – Local Police Athletic Leagues (PAL) conduct a variety of mentor, athletic, educational and cultural programs. Their information can be obtained by calling the police department.

Fraternities – There are five major African American Greek Letter fraternities in the United States. Each organization has approximately 100 years of experience providing service to the community. These organizations consist of college educated Black men that are committed to core principles. They have local chapters in every state and most cities and are mandated to conduct community service. They may be contacted online at www.panhellaniccouncil.com

100 Black men – A national organization composed of professional men committed to the empowerment of the African American community. Their Web site states "100 Black men chapters are educating and empowering youth and families while simultaneously impacting communities." They can be reached at www.100blackmen.org

Local Businesses – The local Chamber of Commerce is the perfect place to start when looking for companies that offer mentor programs and activities. Most companies have an office of community affairs, where they encourage employees to get involved with the local community.

Religious Organizations – Recent decisions to increase funding to religious or faith-based programs have resulted in many churches and mosques offering mentor programs. Contact your local United Way for a list of programs in your community. www.unitedway.org

The reality is that all of the aforementioned organizations are very limited in their ability to find one-on-one mentors. Many of the organizations offer some programs related to African American males. It is important while mothers search for mentors and programs for their sons that they realize "no program is as effective as committed parents." It has been our experience working with boys for the last 15 plus years that usually mothers defer to programs (mentoring, sports- and faith-based). While we support the effectiveness of community-based programs, we can't over estimate the importance of mothers strengthening their relationships with their sons.

One constant theme that we heard throughout our interviews with parents is the maintainence of an open relationship with their sons as they got older. As one parent we interviewed from Los Angeles indicated,

> *I am single mother raising three boys in a gang-infested communities in LA. All of my sons' friends started selling drugs and getting involved in gangs in middle school. Although I worked three part-time jobs, I was committed to going to PTA meetings and making sure my sons knew that no matter how old they got they had to answer to me.*
>
> **Jill, single mother of three
> (Los Angeles, Calif.)**

Over the years in our work with schools, we clearly identify trends in the level of parental engagement. Parents seem to be more engaged in elementary school, but by middle school we see a drastic reduction in parent participation. The majority of research written on child well-being affirms the importance of parents staying connected to their children.

Senior Citizen Centers – Ancient African cultures honored older people by first referring to them as elders, and second by structuring time when the family listened to them recite oral history. Today, many of our seniors do not pass on a history in which they have firsthand knowledge. It is recommended that children have monthly conversations with grandfathers, great uncles and aunts or family members who are considered elders. In addition, it is also recommended that children visit senior citizen homes and engage the elders in conversations about the past. It is important for the boys to have conversations with elders they respect about the origin of the word nigger, why black men were unable to wear belts (history of sagging pants), or "White Only" signs.

PRACTICING FINANCIAL LITERACY

When surveyed about key elements they look for in a mate, women revealed three specific areas. Most women stated that a man should be spiritually guided, family-oriented, and hard working with good credit. Current research suggests that a significant percentage of African American men, ages 24-50, struggle with the later end of the third category. Even when these men are considered hard working, their credit ratings are low. This problem can be linked to little or no education regarding financial literacy.
The United States of America is undergoing one of the worst economic times in its history. Historians and politicians will differ in their opinions on how things got so bad. They also have vast disagreements on how to fix the problem. While both groups are busy blaming each other's failed social and economic policies, the plain truth is that the country, and its citizens, spent more than they made, and saved very little.

American youth generally do not have a good understanding of the role of money in a capitalistic society. The foundation of the American society is money; therefore, it seems out of touch for our youth not to understand money, its role in our society, and how to manage it. Sometime toward the end of the 20th century the U.S. Department of Education started to mandate that children be taught financial literacy as a core part of their curriculum. As a result young people are now expected to know how to identify certain coins by the first grade, add and subtract money by the third grade, calculate percentages by the sixth grade, manage a checkbook by the tenth grade, and maintain good credit by their college years. While most schools are doing their best to teach the basics of financial literacy, most young people who graduate from American schools have a limited understanding of how to manage money. Training at home can have a great impact on a child's general understanding of money.

ENCOURAGE SAVINGS AND INVESTING

I do not pretend to know what President Barack Obama and the other government officials should do to pull the country out of the current financial problems. (My prayers are with him.) Regardless of what they finally decide to do, one thing remains crystal clear: American families will have to tighten their belts, save and invest as much as possible.

While he did not reside with my family, one of the best things my father ever did for me was to give me an $5 a week allowance that was contingent on my behavior and performance in school, home and the community. Before the allowance started, he took me to the bank, taught me the 10 percent rule, and opened a savings account. Every week he would ask what my plans were and he required me to have a solid plan that included:

1. Saving 10 percent (ensuring that I always had money in the bank),
2. Paying for things I needed (this is equal to my bills),

3. Investing for things I wanted (A skate board, baseball cards, electric football men); and

4. Then enjoying myself (candy at the store, money for a movie, Valentine's Day card for little Pamela).

Needless to say $5 went a lot further in the 1970s than it does now, but this general concept worked for me and is a possible first step in teaching young people about savings. We recommend that boys be taught about money as early as possible for a number of reasons. One that stands out the clearest is that money management has a great impact on his ability to be an effective and responsible man, father and husband. We suggest the following:

:: **Teach and reinforce the 10 percent rule** – Savings should be seen as the mandatory first step in financial management. Ten percent of every dollar should be placed in savings before anything else is done. Open a savings account for the boy, provide him with a bank book (or computer pin number), and teach him how to monitor his money.

:: **Provide an allowance that is tied directly to his performance** – Please be clear that we are not suggesting that young people should be paid for doing what they are supposed to be doing. Getting good grades in school, opening the door for senior citizens, and staying awake in church are all things he is supposed to be doing. An allowance should be seen as a weekly lesson that is preparing him to do well in life. Similarly to how a boy is taught to build his mind through reading or to build his body through exercise, so too should he be taught how to manage money. We suggest starting in the sixth grade. The amount provided to him is up to you.

:: **Teach Him How To Pay Bills** – Once at the mall with my son he asked for a toy that I did not have enough money to purchase. When I told him that I did not have enough money he innocently suggested that I go to the ATM and get some more money. This was a clear indication that he had absolutely no idea where money came from! My son was 6 years old at the time so I can excuse him for his youthful exuberance. I, however, often see young men who are in my college courses with a similar mentality about money and paying bills. These young men make purchases such as sneakers, video games and even pizza on credit cards.

The obvious problem here is that they don't realize how they are wrecking their credit and possibly their lives by these foolish purchases. To eradicate these mentalities, it is suggested that parents allow their sons to watch and participate in paying bills. Once they see that a specific time of each day, week or month is used to sit down at the kitchen table and pay bills, they will understand how to do it for themselves. This can start around the same time he is provided an allowance.

:: **Encourage performance-based pay activities** – Due in part to video games and a number of new technologies, today's youth spend more time at home in front of a TV, video game or computer than they do outside. Unlike the 1970s, it is almost impossible to find a kid that is willing to shovel snow in the winter. This leaves an abundance of work for the creative and eager youth who is interested in earning money. As soon as a boy is able to pick up a shovel or rake he should start thinking about mowing the neighbor's lawn or shoveling Ms. Johnson's side walk for pay. Parents are encouraged to support and enforce this thinking in boys as early as possible. Pay for services is so addictive that once a boy receives his first paycheck the parent will never have to ask him to work again.

:: **Make him pay a bill** - Once your son starts to earn money ensure that he pulls his weight and starts to pay at least one bill in the house. This helps him in a number of ways but most importantly it allows him to participate in the family in a more advanced role. The phone bill is a perfect bill because if your son is like most teenagers, the last thing he wants to get cut off is the phone!

Please note that these steps are suggested only as initial steps to teaching financial literacy. A must read book on the next level of financial literacy is Rich Dad Poor Dad by Robert Kiyosaki. In this book, Kiyosaki argues that the lessons taught to him by his dad, and consequently the ones I suggest you consider teaching your son, will actually increase the likelihood of a middle class existence. He argues that by saving 10 percent versus investing will never generate wealth. I believe he is right, however, I also believe that a person must crawl before they can walk, and that is why I suggest considering using the 10 percent rule as the first step in financial literacy.

Searching Your Son's Room

Often we receive numerous e-mails and telephone calls from single parents seeking advice. Many of the questions focus on ways to set limits and boundaries for their sons. Perhaps one of the most frequently asked questions focuses on privacy issues related to searching their son's room and or book bag.
This topic like many others seems to evoke some reservations by parents who believe that their son's room is off limits.

As a rule we believe that searching your son's room and belongings should become a regular routine. Society's dynamics have changed. Society requires parents to work longer hours than ever before.
The days of a 9 to 5 seem to be a relic of the past. For single mothers the juggling of work and family doesn't leave a lot of quality time during the week for mother and son activities. As Renee Wilkerson points out, "I am raising a 15-year old son who I rarely see. We seldom get a chance to spend quality time together due to my crazy work schedule. I have strong reservations about searching my son's room." Ms. Wilkerson like so many other parents is afraid that searching her son's room will some how violate the bonds of trust. While many child and adolescent Psychologist, Pediatricians and other professionals would disagree with the merits of searching your child's room, we firmly believe that parents must be willing to go the extra mile to ensure the safety of the family.

| Raising Him Alone

With this in mind we recommend five rules to consider when searching your son's room. First, make sure you search your son's room when you are sure he is going to be gone for a few hours. During your first search you may need a few hours to determine potential hiding spaces; Second make sure you do not begin cleaning your sons room during the search. No matter how dirty the room may be. Do not clean up anything; Third, place close attention to details and replace everything in exact order and place; Fourth, always assume that your son is capable of not telling you the complete truth; Fifth, be willing to seek advice from friends and family before you confront your son if you find things that may be harmful.

Many parents will read this and assume that searching your son's room violates trust and confidentiality. As Cindy Brown shared with us in a focus group in East Orange, New Jersey, "I decided to search my son's room due to his change in behavior and his fascination with the color blue." Based on the recommendation from a friend who was a former police officer, Ms. Brown searched her son's room. Ms. Brown was amazed to find lots of gang-related (symbols on his walls in his closet, bandanas and handwritten notes) items in his room. Ms. Brown also found a small handgun wrapped in a blue bandana hidden under a box of magazines at the bottom of his closet.

While Ms. Brown's discovery may not be the norm, all too often parents find items that may be disturbing, from pornography to drug paraphernalia.

It is our hope that parents do not find weapons, drugs and other items that may sound the alarm. We believe, however, it is always better to be "ahead of the game."

Finally, we suggest searching coat pockets; stuffed animals; under and inside the mattress; inside a rip of a blanket; pillows; inside light fixtures; inside and underneath dresser drawers; behind dressers; jewelry boxes; band instrument cases; and even CD and DVD cases.

KEEPING HIM SAFE ONLINE

The Internet is a wonderful and exciting tool that has changed the entire landscape. As it relates to young people, the Internet provides unlimited resources that can help in their education, recreation and socialization. Unlike previous generations who had to travel to the library and spend countless hours researching a school project, today's youth are able to sit in the comfort of their rooms and get ten times the amount of work accomplished in half the time. While parents are delighted that their children can complete homework more efficiently, explore research from around the world and even learn a new language, most are surprised and frightened about the "dark side" of the Internet.

There are wide spread reports circulating that outline the dangers of the Internet. Children have been abducted, exposed to inappropriate material, and in some cases they have participated in inappropriate behaviors that would not have been thought of by teenagers a decade ago. Recent reports describe teenagers participating in child pornography through the Internet and the cell phone. A young person takes a picture of himself or herself partially or completely nude and sends it to a friend as some sort of mating ritual. The problem here, among a host of issues, is that once they send the picture, even of themselves, they are guilty of distributing pornography of minors. The two scarier issues are 1) a pedophile may obtain the pictures; and/or 2) they use your computer to send the pictures. The pedophile situation has been seen over and over where a person who preys on children contacts them through the Internet. According to recent U.S. Justice reports, there are thousands of pedophiles and the Internet allows them to engage in these vile behaviors. These reports reveal that there are established groups, clubs and social organizations of adults who use the Internet to meet unsuspecting young people with the intention of starting an inappropriate relationship with them. Luckily for society's sake the government is aware of these monsters and has set up task forces to capture them.

The other concern is when your son inappropriately uses the Internet from your home or office computer. Unfortunately if your son uses your computer to send pictures of a young lady that was sent to him by his friends, the cyberpolice have no way of knowing it is not the adult who owns the computer sending the pictures or videos. Besides disrespecting the young lady, these actions can be deemed criminal and the parent can be arrested for a number of offenses.

Raising Him Alone

How Do We Keep Our Sons Safe on the Internet

Talk with him about his responsibilities. The Internet, cell phones and even video games should be viewed as privileges versus a right. Male children, or all children for that matter, should be made to earn these privileges by demonstrating that they are mature enough to use them. This is similar to when a young person passes the driver education class. Excited and eager to finally get behind the wheel, teenagers must have a long discussion with a parent about vehicle safety. Parents are aware that a single second of inattention, bowing to peer pressure, or just being plain irresponsible can result in fatal injuries and lawsuits. We are suggesting that a similar conversation be held to ensure that male children understand the maturity needed when using these new technologies. We recommend that parents complete a contract with the children about the use of the Internet. Standard items that should be listed in the contract include, but are not limited to:

SAMPLE USE OF TECHNOLOGY CONTRACT

I, _____, promise to behave responsibly while using the Internet, video games, and/or cell phone. I understand how my behavior impacts myself and the people around me and pledge to act in a responsible manner. I also take full responsibility for the use of these items as it relates to my friends.

_____
Child's Name

_____
Child's Signature

_____
Parent Name

_____
Parent Signature

_____
Date

CONSISTENTLY LOOK AT WHAT HE IS DOING

One of the ways the military ensures that soldiers maintain order is the unannounced inspection. As a part of the military culture soldiers are always aware that there may be an inspection of his living quarters, his personal appearance, and even his physical fitness. This culture requires him to address these situations as a part of a daily routine to ensure that he is always in line with expectations. While we do not necessarily suggest using the quarter test on your son's bed every morning (the bed being so tight that a quarter bounces off the sheet when dropped on it), we do suggest regular and unannounced inspections of the technology.

In some homes children may see this as an invasion of their privacy, however, the law (federal, state, local or common sense) does not recognize a child's privacy as it relates to a parent's right to know what his or her child is doing. Moreover, with the average cost of a computer, cell phone and video games, running between $100 and $1,500, the parent must purchase these items so the expectation of privacy is out the window.

Furthermore, failure to know what your child is doing in cyberspace is increasingly viewed as child neglect. It is similar to the parents who had no idea that their sons had stock piles of weapons in their room with the intention of doing something crazy. If not for the sake of the children and their friends, a parent at least needs to be aware of the ramifications of Internet abuse because they will and should be held accountable for what goes on in his or her home.

PARENTAL CONTROL SOFTWARE

Today's youth have found ways, and will continue to find ways to get around the discussions and the family contract. This leaves parents with the option of using software to block inappropriate Internet sites and to monitor their child's behavior online. According to a recent Harvard University study, parents at a minimum should institute the following rules:

1. No chat rooms
2. Only instant messaging with people who the kids know in real life
3. Immediately report any cyberbullying (parents should then contact the parents of the perpetrator)
4. Never give out personal information online
5. Use Web filtering software

THERE IS HELP OUT THERE!

Our research identified more than 100 software products used to block inappropriate sites, limit time children are on the computer, and notify parents of inappropriate use of the Internet. They can be purchased online or at any store that sells computer software (Best Buy, Wal-Mart or Staples). When purchasing software, it is recommended that you go into the store and talk with a sales representative to purchase the product that fits your family's needs. The following is a partial list of software that is available. These programs can be viewed on-line by typing the name provided followed by (.com)

:: PC Pandora®
:: Safe Eyes®
:: NoodleNet ®
:: Net Nanny®
:: Bsafe Online®
:: Sentry At Home®
:: Web Parental Controls®
:: KidsWatch®
:: Besfeonline®
:: Safe Eyes is effective ®
:: iShield® and iShield Pro ®
:: Time's Up®
:: SnoopStick®

Meet the Parents

Inthe acknowledgement of this book, we credited a group of women and in parenthesis we named their sons. These are the single mothers who raised boys on my block. Out of 15 families on my street, 14 were headed by single mothers and 11 of them had male children. No matter how old I get, I will always refer to each of these women as Ms. So and So out of respect. On more than a few occasions I can remember being scolded, loved, and/or generally cared for by each of these women in the same manner as Barbara Stevens (my mom). I was required, as were all of the boys on my street, to introduce myself to my friend's mom. None of us were allowed into their home until our mothers had met. This was done for a number of reasons but specifically to build trust and respect for each other's homes and the community.

My little brother and I resided on the corner and almost every other home belonged to a friend. In the 1970s things were a little different. Children had no need or desire to stay inside the house. In most homes there was only one television and someone's uncle usually had laid claim to it on Saturday afternoon. We, therefore, were made to go outside and play. With no e-mail, texting and/or cell phones, most of the mothers on the block used the old fashion head-out-of–the-window technique to notify their children when dinner was ready.

Using this communication strategy offered each mother an opportunity to maintain a close eye on each child. I was unable to do anything at either end of the block of which my mother was unaware. By the time I got home, somebody's mother would have called my mother to inform her of my actions. This created a community where everyone was accountable to everyone else.

These environments are no longer the norm but are the exception in most American communities. Today most children are not allowed inside their friend's home and when the kids do meet it is usually at a Chuck E. Cheese restaurant, skating rink or some outside function. Quite often, the parents drop the kids off and pick them up without ever going into the establishment. This prevents them from getting to know the children, or more importantly, the parents, with whom their children are socializing. This is unfortunate because not only do parents not meet each other, but the other children do not meet the other parents.

We recommend that all parents meet their peers as well as friends of their sons for two important reasons. First, it sets an important precedent for your child. When he sees his mother socializing with people who are in their inner circle he learns by example. One of the concerns with the new technology is that people have become less sociable. Unlike the days when a young man would meet a girl and request the seven digits (phone number), today's young people simple notify people who may be interested in them to check out their "MySpace" account. While this is cute, it prevents them from talking to each other and consequently hinders their social skills.

Second, meeting the friends of your son let's them know who you are. When his friends know who Ms. Jones is and that she does not tolerate certain things, they are less likely to try to encourage your son to participate in certain at-risk behaviors.

Ten Things You Should Know About Your Son's Friends

1. Name
    a. Why do his parents refer to him as stinky? Does he have a hygiene problem and will that affect

your son's thoughts on personal appearance
2. Address
   a. What neighborhood do they live in? Is it dangerous in that area?
3. Parent's name
   a. Who are his parents? What is their history?
4. Parent's employment
   a. What do his parents do for a living?
5. Parents social affiliations
   a. What social groups do his parents belong to? Are they members of the National Rifle Association? Do they have guns inside their home? Are the guns easily assessable to anyone in the house?
6. Phone Number (home and cell of friends and parents)
   a. How can you contact each of them?
7. Friends e-mail address
   a. Same as above
8. Friends MySpace Account
   a. Same as above
9. Friends Grades
   a. Maybe he can help your son in math
10. Friends Future Aspiration
    a. Positive peer pressure works (most of the time) the same as negative peer pressure. If his friends are studying to go to law school, so too will he.

While some may see this as an intrusion of their son's privacy the information is important to understand with whom your son is spending time.

CHAPTER 2
School House Blues

> My son was diagnosed with attention-deficit hyperactivety disorder (ADHD). This label followed him through elementary school. In his class he is known as the boy on medication. Whenever he gets in trouble his teacher (young white female) always asks him in front of the class did you take your medication?
>
> **Single mother, 3 sons, Dallas, Texas**

Raising Him Alone

Meet the Teacher

Who is teaching your children? Where did they obtain their degree? How are they held accountable for your child's education? These are all questions that every parent has the absolute right to know. In addition to having the right to know, these are things every parent should also see as their duty.

In the Conspiracy to Destroy Black Boys, Jawanza Kunjufu argues that three years of an uninspired teacher can wreck the educational life of a young person. Over the last 10 years, school districts across the country have seen a great number of seasoned educators retire.

> To educate a man is to unfit him to be a slave.
> **Frederick Douglass**

While some districts have been successful in replenishing the vacuum left by these instructors, most are having really tough times. A significant percentage of the best and brightest minds coming out of college are selecting professions that are more lucrative and offer a different set of compensation packages. The lion share of teachers who are entering the profession are doing so as a second or third choice. While most have a general love for teaching, some are primarily concerned with the benefits to themselves. In some states the Department of Education allows people to teach courses that they have absolutely no expertise. As indicated, while most of these people are probably good human beings with the best of intentions, placing them in front of children is similar to going to a heart surgeon that obtained a degree in auto mechanics. I ask again, who is teaching your child?

In *African American Mothers and Urban Schools: The Power of Participation*, Dr. Wendy Glasgow Winters discusses the need for Black mothers to obtain and maintain a consistent presence in their son's education from the start. She reasserts the old adage, "The squeaky wheel gets the oil," meaning that if teachers and administrators realize that a parent is assertively engaged her child's education, they better be as engaged if not more. In addition to keeping the school on notice that she is watching every step, the involved mother also sends the message to the child that she has specific expectations of them. With the onset of new technologies such as e-mail, instant messaging and texting (not to mention the good ole telephone), teachers and parents are able to maintain a level of communication never seen before.

With today's technology a parent's image can even be placed on the big screen, which is available in a growing number of schools, to talk with her child and teacher. She even can be in another part of the world, thus erasing the need to get off of work for parent-teacher meetings.

We suggest parents set a meeting during the summer with the administrator who supervises your child's teacher and the teacher. At this meeting provide contact information and a method to communicate with you consistently. The following are things that you should consider asking:

:: What lessons are my child expected to learn this year?

Raising Him Alone

:: Request weekly updates on how your child is doing on each lesson.
:: What role does homework and at-home activities play in helping my child?

:: Start a daily log that measures your child's progress in each topic.

:: Send your comments to the teacher and request monthly feedback

Under current Title 1 funding each school district is mandated to have this type of reporting system to engage parents in the educational process. Some schools are more advanced than others, but all of them are receiving federal dollars to improve parent participation and must be held accountable as to how they are spending the money. When it comes to your children, we strongly advise that you do not take no for an answer. If your school does not have a suitable reporting system that allows you easy access to the school records and parent-friendly software that you are comfortable with, you can visit www.Linkit.com for information on a software package that accomplishes this goal.

Just Say No To Special Ed

Special Education has become a million dollar business. Although many black boys can benefit from the additional services offered within the public school system, it is essential that parents are aware of the limitations. Parents of Black boys in special education often experience confusion and frustration with the special education process. This process can be intimidating for families who may not be familiar with it.

PARENTS MUST INVESTIGATE THEIR RIGHTS!

According to the Civil Rights Project at Harvard University, young Black males are at greater risk of being disproportionately labeled "mentally retarded." Single mothers raising boys who are placed in special education programs should become experts of the systems.

Each year we receive thousands of calls from mothers whose sons are misdiagnosed and "locked" into special education programs. The following are some basic recommendations for navigating the IEP Process:

:: Understand the IEP Process. IEP stands for Individual Educational Plan. The IEP is developed to provide detailed information for appropriate decisions to be made about your son's educational placement.

:: Prior to the IEP meeting, reach out to an education advocate or teacher that has a back ground in special education. These professionals can help you understand the role of the IEP process.

:: Write down questions and comments that you may have about how your son learns and processes information.

:: Review and understand your options about attending an IEP meeting. Many parents may be unable to attend, based on your work schedule. Review options with the school. Parents may have to schedule a conference call to complete IEP process.

THE DILEMMA WITH SPECIAL EDUCATION

Pam is a 27 year old mother from Gary, Indiana. Pam works two jobs, doesn't not have health insurance and is raising two Black male children. Both of Pam's sons are in special education programs. Pam youngest son, Jiteam is extremely bright but has a problem staying in his seat in school. Jiteam is an energetic, handsome 15 year old. Well liked by his peer, Jiteam is always in the main office.

Jiteam has been diagnosed with ADHD. Pam is getting a lot of pressure from the school social worker, teachers and principal to place her son on medication. Our advice for Pam and the millions of others mothers like Pam: While we believe medication can help in some circumstances, I am concerned with the large number of African American boys who are medicated. Consider these alternative options:

:: Choose diets low in sugar and refined carbohydrate, high in quality protein (your son should not be eating candy and drinking soda). Several studies in the United States of children who have been diagnosed with ADHD show remarkable improvements when the children are placed on diets which eliminate dyes, preservatives and foods commonly associated with allergic reactions (cow's milk, wheat, soy, eggs, corn, chocolate, yeast, orange and apple juice).

:: Increase exercise and physical fitness (Sports- swimming, basketball, football, soccer and others).

:: Increase activities that focus on concentration (Chess, Tai Chi and Yoga).

SINGLE MOTHER RAISING SON WITH A DISABILITY

The following are a few basic tips for mothers raising a son with a disability:

Keep your Eyes on the Prize- Remember That This is Your Son

While your son may have a disability, he is still a human being. Your son still needs your love and support. Love your son and enjoy spending time with him.

CONNECT WITH OTHER MOMS- REALIZE THAT YOU ARE NOT ALONE

So many moms' are in your shoes. The feeling of isolation at the time of diagnosis is almost universal among parents. Get involved with support groups, visit web sites and seek other opportunities to meet others who have a son with a disability.

Language is Important- Learn the Terminology
Learn the language and key terms associated with your son's disability. When speaking to doctors and social workers, you want to be well informed.

Become the Expert- Seek Information
Some mothers accept the diagnosis and the information given by the medical community. Single mothers must become more informed and willing to investigate new research and treatments.

Be strong and assertive- Do Not Be Intimidated
As a single mother, you may feel inadequate at times dealing with the pressures from medical or educational professionals. Do not be intimidated by the educational backgrounds of these and other professionals who may be involved in treating or helping your son. Your son's health and well being is your number one concern.

Develop Thick Skin- Deal with Natural Feelings of Bitterness and Anger. It's natural to feel bitter and even question your spiritual foundation when you give birth to a child with a disability. After you acknowledge your own pain, it's time to "step up" and live for your son.

Keep Your Head Up- Maintain a Positive Outlook
A positive attitude in the long run will help you and your son. Many boys with disabilities have grown up to live productive lives.

Be Resourceful- Find Programs for Your Child
Many programs exist in each state. Be aggressive and don't take "no" for an answer.

Keep it Simple- Keep Daily Routines as Normal as Possible

Maintain normal routines and keep life as simple as possible. This will help your family as you raise a son with a disability.

| Raising Him Alone

Start a Family Book Club

Do you remember the various TV commercials that reinforced lessons such as reading, writing, math and civics? "I'm just a bill. Yes, I'm only a bill. And I'm sitting here on Capitol Hill." This, for some reason, was my favorite commercial. I also remember a Black male character, VERB Man, and I really enjoyed Sesame Street's The Count and Morgan Freeman on The Electric Company. Mr. Rogers was not the manliest character around, so I never got into him too much. All in all, these shows were designed to create a learning environment that consistently, and some would argue, subconsciously, reinforced learning. You might think that with the array of new technologies there would be an abundant amount of new and innovative educational initiatives on TV, but this isn't necessarily the case. Today's youth are bombarded with messages that come quick and hard and are available 24 hours a day – literally.

Youngsters receive information via home phones, cell phones, text messages, email, MySpace, IM and Lord knows what else. While some of the messages and information may be educational, I would venture to say that a significant amount is useless and, in some cases, dangerous.

> The man who has no imagination has no wings.
> **Muhammad Ali**

A recent experience I had with my son motivated me to write this chapter focusing on reading as a family activity. One day while sitting in my living room I noticed that my son had left his cell phone on the end table. I hadn't thought twice about it until it rang and woke me from a Saturday afternoon nap. I picked it up innocently, went to answer it and to my surprise, shock and outright embarrassment the photo ID displayed a picture of a butt naked 15-year-old girl! I angrily answered the phone, and on the other end was what seemed to be an ordinary 15-year-old girl. I asked her if I could speak to her father, and she abruptly hung up and somehow blocked the phone number so I couldn't return the call. My only recourse was to gather myself, go upstairs and start the conversation with my 15-year-old son. We started by talking about how disrespectful it was for him to have this picture of a naked girl on his phone. Then he asked me an honest question which made me stutter and think for a minute before answering. "She sent me the picture. What was I supposed to do?" I had to go downstairs and think for a minute. What would I have done if this happened to me when I was 15? After thinking about it I realized that I would have done the same thing he did, plus send it to all of my friends and brag about being "THE MAN." I went back upstairs to continue the conversation, notifying him of my disapproval and insisting he give me the girl's number. The little girl lived in California. We live in New Jersey. My son met her online. Unfortunately I never got to speak to her father because she somehow disconnected the phone, but I was able to do something constructive with my son. I took away his phone, computer and video game privileges and mandated he read a book. I had recently purchased two copies of Hill Harper's book, "Letters to a Young Brother," so I assigned him the task of reading it. Just like a typical teenager, he tried to be slick and claimed he'd finished in an hour. I knew he was a smart kid but not a speed reader, so I opened my copy of the book and started asking him some questions. I suggested we take turns reading chapters aloud until we finished the book. The chapters were short, which allowed us an opportunity to discuss them by asking three questions:

1. What was the main point of the chapter?
2. What did you find most interesting and why?
3. How can you relate directly to what he had to say?

Chapters 1-3 concentrated on how to confront doubt and fear, how to effectively deal with peer pressure and how to deal with an absent father. These questions, and more importantly our intimate discussion, helped me recognize that my son was:

1. Insecure about meeting girls face-to-face, thus the picture of the little California girl propped up his ego.
2. Uncomfortable approaching girls out of fear of rejection.
3. Succumbing to peer pressure from his friends to see who could obtain the most naked pictures. (I later discovered that he was actually breaking the law because sending pictures of naked kids over the Internet is child pornography. Moreover, if my son uses my computer to send the pictures, I can be brought up on charges.)

Letters to a Young Brother is a MUST READ that we recommend reading with your son. Sending him to the room to read the book on his own won't ensure he gets everything that he should out of it. By reading the book with him you'll learn at what level he's reading, his ability to comprehend what he's reading, and, most importantly, how he connects to what he's reading.

Some other books we suggest reading with your son include:

Doing It My Way: Decision Making for Today's Youth (Matthew Stevens 1998)

Lessons I Learned From My Father (David Miller 2007)

School to Work to Success: A Practical Guide to Finding A Rewarding Career and Enjoying Life (Dale Caldwell, 2008)

The PACT (Sampson, Jenkins and Hunt 2003)

Makes Me Wanna Holla (Nathan McCall 1997)

The following are a few good books for mothers to read:

The Black Parents Handbook for Educating Your Children Outside The Classroom (Baruti Kafele 2004)

Are You Raising One Of The Next Generations of Hoodlums? (Prince O and Dr. Joyce W. Teal 2007)

Boys Into Men (Nancy Boyd Franklin and A.J. Franklin 1993)

African-American Mothers and Urban Schools: The Power of Participation (Wendy Glasgow Winters 1993)

Additionally, please visit www.raisinghimalone.com for a complete list of books we view as "must reads" for single mothers.

TEACH HIM AFRICAN HISTORY

Do you know what year Christopher Columbus discovered America? If you are like most Americans you most likely remember the date because in grade school you were taught to make a rhyme out of the story so you could remember it: Columbus sailed the ocean blue in 1492. We conduct a workshop for students, teachers and parents who teach critical thinking, and the second question we ask after the initial Christopher Columbus question is: What were African-Americans doing in 1492? Most people, sadly even teachers, reply with some far-fetched answer or simply indicate that they don't know. I inform them that there was no such thing as an African-American in 1492, and then I start the workshop by stating "Welcome To Critical Thinking!"

In most schools across the country, young people are being taught how to pass a test rather than how to think critically and how to apply the lessons they're taught. In other words, students are encouraged to look for answers to questions without really understanding the answers. What difference does it make if a young person, especially an African-American, is able to accurately remember the dates things happened if he or she is unable to relate his or her existence to these dates? In this case, the information learned becomes irrelevant.

Making education relevant is one of the essential methods to ensure young people learn. Noted scholars that have been referenced throughout this book like Molefe Asante, Na'im Akbar, Lenworth Gunther, Baruti Kafele and Joy Leary all suggest that today's youth require Knowledge of Self in order to succeed in school, and, for that matter, life.

An easy way to start this process is by talking with young men about themselves, their family and their history. What is your son's name? My name is Matthew Paul Stevens. My mother indicates that the name was designed by combining my grandparents' names, Mattie and Paul. Later in life I was told that Matthew meant "Gift From God." This knowledge has helped me throughout life by providing a foundation of greatness. Common wisdom says God gives only good gifts, therefore, by virtue of my name alone I should be good to go. Does your son know what his name means? A conversation about his name can be fun, engaging and can also help him realize he is unique and special. Most American names don't have a formal meaning, but as you can see by the way my mother put two names together to come up with one, you don't need a formal meaning if you had a reason for selecting the name. Hardly anyone selects a name randomly, so no matter what you have named your child, there's an interesting history behind the story, history that should be explained to him as a fortifying brick in his self foundation.

After explaining your rationale for his name, another exercise to expand the conversation and teach him its relevance is What's in a Name Game. The tools needed for the game are large pieces of paper for each family member, writing tools, dictionaries and/or thesauruses and good senses of humor.

Directions: Write your name from top to bottom on the paper as indicated below:

M
A
T
T

Using the dictionary or thesaurus, list a noun, verb and adjective that describes you for each letter. The key here is to be able to tell a story supporting your claim to the letter. For example, M stands for Motivated Man on a Mission. Using this example I must justify:

1. Why I am qualified to refer to myself as a man.
2. How I have demonstrated motivation and
3. My mission

The same things should be done for each letter. The goal of the game is to require your son to design his own meaning for his name. This helps him with his self esteem by identifying what he's good at, allowing him to exude confidence and continue growing.

Please note the What's in a Name Game is designed as a family activity that should be played accordingly. Once your son sees your example two things will happen:

1. He will follow your lead and fully, actively participate and

2. He most likely will learn something new about his mother and recognize a few things he has in common with her.

After discussing the history of your son's name, it is a good practice to go into the basement, pull out old photo albums and have a family discussion about the people, places and events in the pictures.

This can be a fun and engaging activity designed to help young men recognize the richness in their family history. Furthermore, when they see their resemblance in a picture of Great, Great, Great Grandpa, they can also start to understand how history connects all things. Even some of your more notorious relatives can be mentioned and discussed during these activities as a way to point out how mistakes may have shaped a person's life. It is quite all right to learn from someone else's mistakes so that history does not repeat itself. After conducting this activity, take a picture of you and your son and put it in the album as a reference to a learning moment in both of your lives: The Day We Started Our Journey To Self.

FROM SELF TO BEYOND

One of the greatest orators, leaders and historical giants in America was Malcolm X. Early in the 1960's he predicted that the youth of that generation would be the ones to finally see through some of America's hypocrisy and begin to fight for their human rights. Upon his return from Mecca, he hinted at a psychological and spiritual return to Africa as a prerequisite for Black people to gain the frame of mind necessary to improve their situation. Malcolm was assassinated shortly after that, some say because of a rift he was having with the Nation of Islam at the time. However, others believe his insistence that African people throughout the world unite and fight against imperialism was the real reason he was killed. Malcolm himself feared his insistence would possibly cause his death. However, why he was killed is far more important than who killed him.

Has your son read The Autobiography of Malcolm X? If not, it is mandatory reading for Black males. It was not mentioned in the Start A Family Book Club because this is a book that a young man should read on his own, around age 14. We recommend giving the book (not the movie) as an 8th grade graduation gift to your son. He should be assigned the task of reading the book and doing a report on it during the summer before he enters high school so he arrives ready to start his journey armed with some of the next Knowledge of Self levels: How our ancestors have paved the way for us. One of the books suggested in the Family Reading Club was Makes Me Wanna Holla (Nathan McCall, 1989). It is designed to prepare your son to be ready to experience The Autobiography of Malcolm X. McCall's life story is more in line with an average African-American brother, and reading it first may provide young men with a better understanding of how certain things in their lives are helping mold them. McCall, like most educated African-American men, refers to Malcolm X as a molding force in his life. He, like many, read the book in prison and credits it with turning his life around. Our sincere hope is that your son can read and be inspired by this book in his room rather than in a cell. Several Internet-based resources are available to assist in discovering African-African-American history. Encyclopedia Africana is one of the leading Web sites designed to provide more information about our history please visit

| *Raising Him Alone*

www.africanaencyclopedia.com.

In addition to reading books, one of the best ways to teach African history is orally. Require your son to talk to elders! What does your grandfather or oldest living relative think about Barack Obama being elected President of the United States? I wish my grandfather could have lived to see it. I would have liked to hear some of the stories about how life was for him growing up in this country. When a youngster hears his relatives talk about the past it can have a great impact on how he sees the future. African history is world history and important to all human beings to understand. It is crucial that our young men learn, and most importantly understand, African history as it relates to them, their family, the community, this country and the world.

The following are 20 African/African-American males you should expose your son to:

Marcus Garvey
Kwame Nkrumah
David Walker
Bob Marley
Booker T. Washington
Steven Biko
Frederick Douglass
Paul Robeson
Malcolm X
Bob Johnson (Former BET owner)
Langston Hughes
Ralph Ellison
W.E.B. Du Bois
Mickey Leland
Benjamin Banneker

Raising Him Alone

John Henrik Clarke
Martin Luther King Jr.
Adam Clayton Powell
James Baldwin
Thurgood Marshall

Finally, we strongly suggest you plan some field trips that expose your son to African-/African-American history:

Schomburg Center
www.schomburgcenter.org

Motown Historical Museum
www.motownmuseum.com

The King Center
www.thekingcenter.org

The National Civil Rights Museum
www.civilrightsmuseum.org

National Great Blacks in Wax Museum
www.ngbiwm.org

Negro Leagues Baseball Museum
www.nlbm.com

TEACH HIM A NEW LANGUAGE

One of the coolest things about President Barack Obama is his mastery of not only the English language but of French and other languages. In 2008 when he was challenged to go to Europe to gain foreign-speaking experience, he did an excellent job in expressing his thoughts to people of all nationalities. Today's youth from all over the world, and particularly young black men, now have an example of the proper way to speak. For a minute, people all over the world must have thought Americans were not intelligent and did not have a mastery of even their own language.

That's in part because President Bush made a number of mistakes during his eight years in the White House, and some of his quotes have become legendary material for late-night comics. Anyone anywhere in the world who heard him speak on the nightly news most likely gained a negative first impression of how Americans communicate, based on the speaking skills of its leader. As far as African-Americans are concerned, we, too, have had our problems regarding communicating to the public. Most of our boys seem as if they are addicted to the phrase "Ya Know What I'm Sayin?" A clear indication that your son may need language intervention is if he repeats this phrase after every third word. Ed Lover, a radio host on New York City's 101.5 FM Morning Show, used to ring a bell every time a guest uttered this phrase to get our young people, especially the ones who get the opportunity to grace the airwaves, to see that WE DON'T KNOW WHAT YOU ARE SAYIN!

Our hope is that President Obama will lead the way to helping Americans regain respect around the world with his examples of elegance and intelligence. Parents can help by ensuring their children take a foreign language course in school. I recently saw on the news that a town in the southwest part of the country was mandating Spanish be taught as a secondary language so Americans could communicate with the majority of the Spanish-speaking population in that town. While I am bothered by the fact that so many Spanish-speaking people entered the country illegally, I am also a realist and understand that their presence in this country is no mistake. If the government wanted illegal immigration to stop, it could implement steps immediately to put an end to it. These folks have been brought here, in some cases, for a reason! While it is easy to stop illegal immigration, it is not that easy and may not even be possible, to return all of these people to their original country. Therefore, we are stuck together and must find a way to coexist.

One of the ways Black people can ensure their survival in this country is to learn how to speak Spanish. In addition to being able to say hola to Jose, the baker, this skill may actually be needed to get a job in the near future. The next time you go to McDonalds take a look at who is working there. Not too many Black people are applying for those jobs, and if the trends continue, one might have to be able to speak Spanish to work in even these types of establishments. As a percentage of the population, Spanish people in America are having more children than anyone else, and due to this fact (2007 Census) they will be the largest minority group in the next few decades. If Black people do not learn how to speak Spanish, they will limit their opportunities in the current, and possible future, job markets.

| *Raising Him Alone*

CHAPTER 3
Navigating the Hood

(Game Recognizes Game)

No matter what the circumstances of conception, your body was chosen to bring forth this child of God. Even if the father doesn't tell you, "Remember you are worthy of respect and love." Keeping my grandson's safe is a full time job for me. We live in a tough community. I worry every day.

Single grandmother of three, Mobile, AL.

| *Raising Him Alone*

Teaching Him How to Defend Himself

Recently while my son was on a playground near our house, I allowed him to play with some boys we didn't know. It is always amazing watching the interaction between young boys. My son was 8 at the time and the other boys were close to his age. As I along with the three other parents watched the "bonding ritual" occur among the boys, I knew it was only a matter of time before things got physical. In the male world, 90 percent of the time when boys get together sooner or later wrestling, slap boxing and other forms of bravado begin to surface. As we all looked on I realized I would have to explain to the mothers with sons what was about to happen. Within a few minutes, two of the boys who knew each other started grabbing and tussling with each other. Minutes into the exchange one of the boys challenged my son. The other parent yelled, "No, Michael. You are too big to wrestle with him." My son replied, "Daddy is it okay?" I was somewhat reluctant at first because my son, although small in stature, had already learned how to defend himself as well as how to neutralize potentially dangerous situations. You see, my son had already been involved in martial arts Tai Chi and wrestling. Needless to say, he already had a great understanding of his natural abilities, balance and offensive and defensive techniques.

Although only 8, my son had already begun to master levels of self discipline and a greater understanding of the importance of self defense. As the boys began to wrestle, I quickly realized how important it is for mothers to get their sons involved in physical activities. It seems we are producing a generation of boys who are not physically fit due to the alarming amount of time they spend on videos versus running sprints, climbing trees and playing outside. Some of this, in part, is due to mothers' fears of allowing their sons to be outside with the "neighborhood boys." While safety must always be a priority, mothers must be willing to allow their sons to interact with boys who may be rough and tough. This interaction will teach your son some very valuable lessons that he will be able to apply in all areas of his life.

> I don't know the key to success, but the key to failure is trying to please everybody.
> **Bill Cosby**

At a time when so many boys are confronted with school bullies and the challenges of traveling from one neighborhood to another just to get to school, it is important for boys to have basic self-defense skills. Based on much of the research that we conducted for the book, issues related to bullying are often overlooked. Being bullied has become a matter of life and death. Thousands of school-aged boys are subjected to bullying on a regular basis. Often this bullying is manifested in school-yard fights, threats of repeated violence and students missing days from school – likely from fear of being bullied.

In November 2006 Timothy Oxedine, a 14-year-old student at Lemmel Middle School in Baltimore, MD., was charged as an adult for the murder of Markel Williams, 15. Published reports indicate that Oxedine was the victim of repeated bullying from Williams and other boys in the school. The Oxedine case is another glaring example of the seriousness of school bullying and school violence. According to numerous studies, 80 percent of adolescents reported being bullied

during their school years, and 90 percent of kids in 4th through 8th grade report being victims of bullying. Often the boys who are bullied lack self confidence and the ability to confront aggression. We believe that martial arts and other sports are critical in teaching boys self confidence. The following are some suggested programming for your son:
Enroll your son in martial arts courses such as Tai Chi, Yoga, Karate and Jujitsu, which teach him how to defend himself.

Allow your son to play contact sports such as football, basketball, wrestling and boxing.
Monitor your son's activities outside of school and during non-school hours, as bullying often occurs during this time.

Discuss bullying and violence with your son. It will create an environment which allows your son to discuss issues that may be occurring. Often boys will not admit to their parents that they are being bullied.

DATING – TEACH HIM HOW TO TREAT A LADY

Among the basic lessons mothers hope boys will learn are the importance of honoring and respecting women. This is perhaps one of the most important lessons – and the most difficult. In today's society unlike with previous generations, boys and girls are socialized by numerous media outlets and technology which don't always honor and respect girls and women.

| *Raising Him Alone*

Whether it's the hyper-sexed reality TV shows like Flavor of Love with Flavor Flav or ABC's Bachelor – Joe Millionaire, America's fascination with sexuality has greatly influenced youth. To add to this, musical portrayals of young males having multiple sex partners, driving expensive cars and travelling by jet seem to be the dominant themes in a large percentage of Rap and R&B singles that make Billboard's Top 10.

Over time, music has come a long way in shaping the values of generations of children, youth and young adults. I can vividly remember LL Cool J's I Need Love on his Bigger and Deffer album, which expressed his love for a young lady. The year was 1987, and LL Cool J's message of finding love was on the minds and hearts of teenagers during the late 1980s. In the opening lyrics, LL Cool J shares with us his innermost thoughts:

> *When I'm alone in my room sometimes I stare at the wall*
> *And in the back of my mind I hear my conscience call*
> *Telling me I need a girl who's as sweet as a dove*
> *For the first time in my life, I see I need love*

Today we are far removed from hearing songs that talk about love, intimacy and respect. For single mothers raising boys, it is essential that making sure boys understand the importance of honoring and respecting girls and women becomes a priority in your home. The values that you teach your son will be exhibited in how he treats girls and women when he is not around you. This must be an ongoing conversation with your son due to the graphic nature and portrayal of girls and women in the vast majority of music videos that air in most markets.

Raising Him Alone

In a recent report titled The Rap on Rap, the Parents Television Council found an alarming amount of offensive/adult content in the three music-video shows it monitored on BET and MTV during periods in December and March. The report found that children watching BET's Rap City and 106 & Park and MTV's Sucker Free on MTV were bombarded with adult content – sex, violence, profanities or obscenities – once every 38 seconds. This report, like numerous others in years past, highlights the power the media has in projecting images to young people. While we know that parents have the option to turn off the television, it appears that boys and young men are being bombarded with images of sex and sexuality on a regular basis.

It is important for mothers to watch and discuss the television shows and videos to which our sons are exposed. Mothers have an obligation to help boys understand how to treat girls/women. This cannot be left up to men!

In February 2009, 19-year-old R&B singer Chris Brown was arrested following a domestic violence incident. While speculation continues over the incident, his arrest raises questions about teen dating and relationships. Often when people hear the term domestic violence, they automatically think about adults.

The following facts underscore the need for mothers to make sure they are having serious, ongoing conversations about dating and relationships with their sons:

:: 58 percent of rape victims report being raped

| *Raising Him Alone*

between the ages of 12-24

:: 77 percent of female and 67 percent of male high school students endorse some form of sexual coercion, including unwanted kissing, hugging, genital contact and sexual intercourse.

:: In 9 out of 10 rapes in which the offender is under 18, so is the victim.

We hope these statistics highlight the seriousness of dating and violence associated with dating and relationships.

Tips for teaching boys ways to respect girls/women:

Always be a gentleman – be polite, nice and respectful even if she doesn't respect herself.

Communicate in a respectful way – avoid cursing and use of language that you know is not appropriate. (Speak to her the same way you would want a man speaking to your mother.)

Be yourself – this will impress her more than anything else you can do. You don't have to show off in front of your friends.

Become friends – get to know her likes and dislikes. Sure you think she's the prettiest girl in school, but is that all you want to know about her?

Under no circumstances should you ever hit a girl/woman – this includes pushing or grabbing her violently.

The company you keep – avoid being around or hanging with boys/young men who are disrespectful and/or violent toward girls/women.

Keeping our sons out of the criminal justice system

What happens if your son gets jammed up? (My son has been arrested.) Often, a parent's worst nightmare is getting a call in the middle of the night saying his/her child has been arrested. Yet, this scenario happens to so many unsuspecting parents each year. Keeping Our Sons Out of the system seeks to ease the pain of so many parents by providing information that can assist families in the process of navigating the juvenile justice system. With African-American youth representing a large part of the juvenile system, our goal is to empower parents to advocate for their children based on informed decisions about parental rights, understanding the court process and the role of legal counsel. The following are just a few things that parents should consider:

Twenty-one Critical Questions for Parents

:: *Do you know all of your child's friends?*
:: *How often do you search your child's room?*
:: *Does your child have issues resolving conflicts without resorting to violence?*
:: *How does your child respond to authority figures?*

Raising Him Alone

- :: How does your child respond to peer pressure?
- :: Does your child have a MySpace or Face book page and/or regular access to the Internet?
- :: What subjects does your child struggle with in school?
- :: Has your child been suspended or expelled? (If yes, why?)
- :: Have you caught your child stealing or lying to you within the last six months?
- :: Do you know whether your child smokes marijuana?
- :: Have you ever requested a drug test for your child?
- :: How often do you get calls from your child's school about fights and other disturbances?
- :: Does your child associate with youth involved in gangs?
- :: What kind of music and/or TV programming does your child like?
- :: Does your child play video games? (If so, which ones and how often?)
- :: Has your child ever gotten in trouble for bullying and/or picking on other children?
- :: Has your child ever been caught with a weapon (knife, box cutter, gun, etc.?)
- :: How often does your child make bad choices which could cause self harm and/or harm to others?
- :: What kind of tattoos does your child have? (Do you know what the tattoos mean?)
- :: How often does your child threaten or blame siblings for issues that occur at home?
- :: How often does your child disobey house rules (curfew)?

10 Rules of Survival When Stopped by Police

> Nothing in the world is more dangerous than sincere ignorance and consciencious stupidity.
> **Rev. Dr. Martin Luther King, Jr.**

For single mothers raising boys, many daily lessons must be taught to ensure that our community is able to produce sober, responsible and spiritually guided men. The harsh reality is that our sons, as they get older, will get stopped and detained by police.

On Jan. 1, 2009, an unarmed young Black male was shot and killed on the Bart Subway platform in Oakland, Calif., by the police. The videotaped killing of Oscar Grant sparked riots in and around the Oakland community. Grant's murder is another glaring example of why we need to prepare our sons to deal with a police stop.

In every community, police officers are generally depicted as community or public servants, but in many communities police officers are viewed as your worst enemy. Over the last 10-15 years we have seen a rise in police brutality cases. These issues have included but are not limited to police misconduct, which includes false arrests, intimidation, racial profiling, political repression, surveillance abuse, sexual abuse and police corruption.

We have seen footage and read stories about numerous young Black males who have been victimized by the police. At the end of the day, mothers must teach their sons the "rules of engagement" when stopped by the police.

The following are some basic rules that you can teach your son to assist him when he is stopped by the police.

1. Be polite and respectful when stopped by the police.
2. Stay calm and remain in control. Watch your words, body language and emotions.
3. Don't, under any circumstances, get into an argument with the police.
4. Always remember that anything you say or do can (and most likely will) be used against you in court.
5. Keep your hands in plain sight and make sure the police can see your hands at all times.
6. Avoid physical contact with the police. Do not even brush against them in any manner.
7. Do no run, even if you are afraid of the police.
8. Even if you believe you are innocent, do not resist arrest.
9. Don't make any statements about the incident until you are able to meet with a lawyer or public defender.
10. Remember that your goal is to get home safely.

Use the above rules to help you do that. If you feel that your rights have been violated, you and your parents have the right to file a formal complaint with your local police jurisdiction.

Your son is arrested – Parental Rights

According to Building Blocks for Youth, a policy and advocacy group in Washington, D.C., Black and brown youth are disproportionately arrested. For

| *Raising Him Alone*

example, although African-American youth ages 10 to 17 constitute 15 percent of their age group in the U.S. population, they account for **26 percent** of juvenile arrests, **32 percent** of delinquency referrals to juvenile court, **41 percent** of juveniles held in delinquency cases, **46 percent** of juveniles in corrections institutions and **52 percent** of juveniles transferred to adult criminal court after judicial hearings.

For this reason, we believe that it is important for parents to understand the court process as well as general information on things to do if their sons are arrested. Whether your son is 3-years-old or 13-years-old, this information may become useful to you and/or other single mothers in your network.

Step 1

Find out about the charges against your son. What is your son specifically charged with? The police have a responsibility to inform you (parent/guardian/caregiver) immediately if your son has been arrested and to tell you why he is being held.

Step 2

Hire an attorney, one with a background in juvenile crime. Your attorney can give you an in-depth explanation of local laws concerning these rights. You may have to give your attorney a retainer, or a lump sum of money, so he'll begin working on your case.

| *Raising Him Alone*

Step 3

Discus in detail your son's charges. Is your child being charged as an adult or as a minor? His rights may vary based on the charges, and your attorney will explain the implications of being tried as an adult versus a minor.

Step 4

Learn whether you'll be held liable for your son's behavior. In some states, parents are required to pay restitution to victims for their son's crime.

Contact the American Civil Liberties Union (ACLU) to find out whether the rights of your child have been violated (see resources below). The ACLU exists to help those who aren't familiar with the law understand and receive their fundamental rights, as guaranteed by The Constitution.

Follow up by asking whether your son's court records will be available to the public. Some states may not allow juvenile records to be accessed by anyone except juvenile officials; others may allow educational institutions and prospective employers to have access to these records.

**Once he's arrested, the police must immediately notify the minor's parents, guardian or caretaker of the arrest. The minor is allowed two phone calls, to a parent and an attorney. If the officer decides on detention, he must take the minor before a probation officer within 24 hours of his arrest.

Keeping Your Son Out of a Gang

The issue of gangs has been identified as one of the most urgent challenges facing young males. Often, boys join gangs as a means to define manhood to connect with older male role models. For this reason, we have developed some basic information about gang identification for parents. Recently while in Savannah, Ga., speaking at a conference, I suggested to parents and teachers that one of the keys to keeping boys out of gangs is reaching them early. By as early as the second and third grade in many communities, boys begin to learn about gangs. For this reason, single mothers cannot wait until their sons are in middle school to begin educating them on the dangers of gangs. We believe the best way to keep our sons out of gangs is to make sure we develop clear lines of communication and monitor all of their activities. Much of the information contained in Chapter 1, There's No Place Like Home, can help strengthen the bond between mothers and sons. Monitoring friends, searching your son's room and creating standards in your home can reduce the likelihood that your son will join a gang.

**Please note that many gangs are recruiting boys in elementary school. Often parents think issues related to gangs don't arise until middle or high school.

For additional information on gangs and things parents can do, please visit http://www.gangwar.com/dynamics.htm.

Bloods
:: Considered one of the largest street gangs in the United States.
:: Gang initiations vary from getting beaten up to participating in a crime.
:: Colors are red, black, brown and pink.
:: Usually are seen wearing bandanas and wave caps with the colors red, black brown and pink.
:: Tattoos vary, but the most popular is the dog paw made up of three dots (looks like a triangle made of three dots.)

Crips
:: Well-established across the United States.
:: Known for involvement in drug distribution and violent acts against rival gang members.
:: Colors are blue, gray, orange and purple.
:: Six-pointed Star of David symbol.

Gangster Disciples
:: Chicago-based, same-gender street gang which has, over the years, grown into one of the largest criminal organizations in the U.S.
:: Originally formed on the south side of Chicago, they now have an enormous presence in that city and in other Midwest cities such as Milwaukee, Minneapolis and Gary, IN.
:: Within the last five or so years, evidence of Gangster Disciples has increasingly been discovered in the southern part of the U.S.
:: Symbols include a Six-pointed Star of David, in remembrance of its co-founder "King" David Barksdale. (There is no connection to the Jewish symbol apart from the name of King David.)
:: A three-pointed pitchfork pointed upward like the letters psi (displaying it upside-down is considered an insult).

:: A love heart with wings, horns and a tail.
:: Colors are black and flue.

Selecting the Right Coach

It is well documented that sports play a pivotal role in the lives of boys. Whether it's football, basketball, soccer, swimming or any of the other recognized sports, these activities play an enormous role in the physical, psychological and social development needs of boys. While millions of boys throughout the U.S. participate in organized sports, seldom do we find parents taking an active role in researching sporting teams and their coaches. Often, single mothers in their quest to find male role models for their sons gravitate toward sports. While using sports as a meaningful activity for boys can be beneficial, it is essential that parents interview perspective coaches. At a time when professional scouts are looking at promising athletes at the Amateur Athletic Union (AAU) and Pop Warner levels, parental participation and monitoring are important.

Recently I decided to research newspaper archives and YouTube videos to find incidents involving youth in sports, and their parents. I was not surprised to find numerous altercations between parents and coaches and parents and referees. In Corpus Christi, Texas, at a Pee Wee football game, a parent threw a coach to the ground over a disagreement, igniting a brawl involving numerous parents from both teams. The video shows mothers kicking other parents who were trying to break up the fight. At a soccer match in L.A., more than 30 parents and coaches clashed in a fight that ended in the arrest of three adults. Two parents were taken to the hospital, one parent needed treatment for minor cuts and a swollen eye and another suffered a two-inch bite on his arm.

Although many would agree that sports has a variety of positive benefits, including physical conditioning, sportsmanship and teaching boys to work together as a team, parents should be concerned about the highly competitive nature of youth sports. The competitiveness has been heavily influenced by the illusion so many youth and their parents have about a professional career. Kevin Hart, a fun-loving high school football player from a small town in Nevada, was recently featured on ESPN's Outside the Lines, which covers news and opinions related to sports. Kevin's feature story is a glowing example of the impact that competitive sports has on the psyche of young, promising athletes. Kevin, a 6'5" 290-pound senior lineman, held a press conference at his school announcing he would be playing Division 1 football for the University of California. When the smoke cleared, Kevin's family and teammates were stunned to learn the whole story was fabricated.

Stories like Kevin Hart's are not uncommon; the quest for boys to become celebrated hometown heroes is prevalent. For this reason, we believe parents must take a more-active role in selecting coaches and sporting programs that focus on the following areas:

- :: Moral development
- :: Sportsmanship
- :: Losing with dignity
- :: Physical and mental fitness
- :: Honoring authority and respecting leadership

Finally, we believe the following questions are key for parents to ask when choosing a team and coach:

- :: How important are honesty and character in your coaching philosophy?
- :: What are your coaching credentials (Most organized sports teams require coaches to participate in training and seminars).
- :: What percentage of your players graduate and go to college?
- :: What is the team's policy for students who struggle academically?
- :: Does the team have a written code of conduct for players and coaches?
- :: How many weekly practices are held and what is the duration of each practice?

CHAPTER 4
Protecting the King
(Health & Wellness)

We live in a tough neighborhood in Gary. I work two jobs during the week and part-time at a dry cleaners on the weekends to make ends meet. The last thing on my mind was taking my kids to the doctor. Two years ago I learned my lesson. My son had a bad infection in his foot due to a cut that went untreated.

**Single mother of six,
Gary, IN.**

| *Raising Him Alone*

Expect him to take care of himself

> My father taught that the only helping hand you're ever going to be able to rely on is the one at the end of your sleeve.
> **J. C. Watts, Jr.**

In early chapters in the book we provide mothers with strategies to protect the emotional lives of their sons. While this is important, it is also important to make sure that we protect the physical essence of our sons.

We have identified three areas: Adequate sleep; Exercise and Sports and Coping with Stress as critical areas to help boys take care of themselves.

ADEQUATE SLEEP

Boys are notorious for "burning the midnight oil." Whether it's talking on the phone to some little girls and/or playing video games, boys love to stay up late. Your son is probably no exception. Conventional wisdom suggests your son doesn't need a lot of sleep because he is still young. The reality is that boys (teens) need about nine hours of sleep a night to maintain the day-to-day routines of being a teen. Often many boys in high school juggle part-time jobs, homework, school activities and friends.

Many of the single mothers that we interviewed for the book suggested that their sons were not on a schedule when it comes to going to bed during the week or weekend. We recommend that you and your son develop a schedule for bedtime, recognizing it may change, at times, because of special events and other things that may occur. Identifying and following a set bedtime may mean prioritizing extracurricular activities, limiting time spent on the telephone, the computer and on other social outlets that may cause boys to stay up late.

EXERCISE & SPORTS

While sports and exercise are recommended for growing boys, it is important for parents to monitor these activities. Each year we get reports about teens passing out and dying as a result of heat strokes and dehydration. Boys who play outdoor sports requiring practice during the height of the summer (football, soccer, track and field) are at the greatest risk for health-related problems.

Many times boys who are involved in team sports are more concerned with competing than taking care of their own bodies. Mothers should discuss these issues with their sons to ensure they are aware of the warning signs. Mothers should also encourage their sons to pay attention to early signs and symptoms of dehydration, including:

:: Dry or sticky mouth
:: Thirst
:: Headache
:: Dizziness
:: Cramps
:: Excessive fatigue

COPING WITH STRESS

Growing up without a father can be stressful enough. When you add school work and making friends to the equation, coping with stress can be difficult for boys and young males. Talking to your son and making him aware of the challenges boys face in

| Raising Him Alone

society, particularly young Black and Latino males, is important. Teach him about dealing with racism, prejudice and racial profiling.

Keep Him Smiling
(Taking Your Son to the Dentist)

Deamonte Driver should be a household name among parents. Deamonte, a 12-year-old from Washington, D.C., died Feb. 25, 2007, because of complications from an untreated, abscessed tooth. The infection spread to his brain, and he died despite two brain surgeries and a lengthy hospital stay. We first became familiar with Deamonte while speaking at a parent summit in Trenton, N.J.

Marian Wright Edelman, President and Founder of The Children's Defense Fund, was the featured speaker at the summit. On stage she had a large poster with Deamonte's picture to symbolize the importance of health and dental care to the capacity crowd.

Deamonte's untimely death sent shockwaves through the medical community because a simple set of dental procedures could have saved his life. His death is a wakeup call to parents that dental care must be a priority. Greater efforts by parents can ensure many dental issues are prevented. At a time when healthcare in the U.S. is in serious trouble, more than 100 million Americans lack dental insurance. This dramatically impacts a child's ability to receive adequate dental care.

| *Raising Him Alone*

According to the Centers for Disease Control and Prevention's National Center for Health Statistics, kids miss an estimated 51 million school hours annually because of oral health problems. This data is particularly troubling when we think about the overall health status of young Black males. The Raising Him Alone campaign realizes the importance of healthy children. For this reason we believe that developing dental practices is critical for boys.

Although insurance may be an issue, parents should investigate community based clinics and other health-related resources. Often dental services exist for children that go underutilized by families.

Parents on a fixed income should investigate dental services that are free or offered on a sliding-fee scale. Parents can begin by contacting their local social services department.

The following are a few basic tips for mothers raising boys:

TOOTH BRUSHING

Start cleaning your son's teeth as soon as they come through the gums. Enforce tooth brushing after breakfast and before bedtime so that it becomes part of your son's daily routine.

As your son gets older you can teach him how to brush his own teeth, using a gentle, circular motion and fluoride toothpaste. Make sure he understands he has to clean every tooth.

TOOTHPASTE

Most toothpaste contains fluoride, which has been proven to protect against decay. Fluoride is also Added to the water supply in some parts of the country. In these areas, tooth decay has been significantly reduced.
Parents should also investigate all-natural toothpastes like Tom's.

GOING TO THE DENTIST

It's a good idea to take your son to the dentist when you go for your own routine check-ups, even when he is too young to have teeth. This helps him to become familiar with the importance of going to the dentist.

Your dentist will recommend check-ups at intervals suitable for your son, who should be excited about going to the dentist! Frequent check-ups help your dentist treat decay early before it causes toothaches or more serious problems. (Remember Deamonte Driver.)

For more information on basic dental care for children and teens please visit www.simplestepsdental.com.

The Sex Talk with Your Son

Recently while speaking at a conference in Atlanta, I was approached by several mothers who shared the same concern. This encounter was typical of the many we get while speaking to groups: Being approached by single mothers who are raising boys and who are struggling to understand the "Boys code." In case you don't know, the Boys code is a set of rituals and practices adopted by boys and often understood only by boys and the men in their lives. Each mother seemed a little uncomfortable as one of them began to "beat around the bush," rambling about doing the best she can to raise her son alone. As she spoke, the other mothers nodded their heads in agreement. I finally interrupted her and asked what age she began talking to her son about sex.

While we are not medical doctors, we believe the conversation should be based on age and your son's maturity level. Most experts suggest beginning this conversation at 8, but we feel starting as young as 4 may not be out of the question. We acknowledge many parents will be uncomfortable having this conversation, but we feel it is critical for mothers. It is our hope that after reading this you will consult your son's pediatrician as well as find books in the library or on the Internet to reinforce our recommendations.

We suggest your conversation begins with "good touch" and "bad touch" even if your son is older than 8. This conversation should have occurred when your son was around 4, but we cannot take things for granted. Many parents are afraid to have this conversation with their sons for fear of scaring them. Although difficult and uncomfortable for many parents to discuss, this may be even more difficult for single mothers raising boys. This information from mothers represents the greatest tool to prevent sexual abuse.

It is important for us to cite a few things that often are not discussed:

- Male victims of sexual abuse constitute an extremely under-identified, under-served and frequently misunderstood population.
- In urban communities sexual abuse is not discussed, rather it's almost viewed as taboo.
- One out of six boys is a victim of sexual abuse.
- In one study of 30 male victims of sexual abuse, the average age at the first time of abuse was 8 years, 4 months.

The aforementioned information underscores the need to talk about what is appropriate and what's not appropriate with your son.

When discussing the topic of sex with your son it is essential to begin by letting him know you want to be able to have an open and honest conversation. Mothers should also tell their sons that although it may be difficult for a boy to discuss sex with his mother, it's important for his own health and safety. Mothers should begin with suggested topics like masturbation (touching yourself), being attracted to another person, kissing, oral sex and STDs. As we stated earlier, your son's age and maturity should determine the content of the discussion.

The following are four quick tips for parents:

Admit to your son that sex is a great thing.
However, explain the risks associated with sexual intercourse. Also, discuss the importance of learning

about his body and being able to discuss his body parts with his parents before considering sex.

Spend time making sure you and your son read about his body parts. It seems many parents find it easier to talk to girls about sex than boys. Often girls are given far more information about sex than boys. Topics like having an erection or wet dreams are things mothers must be willing to discuss. These issues can't be left up to your son's peer group to discuss.

WHAT ARE YOUR SON'S FRIENDS SAYING ABOUT SEX?

Perhaps one of the most important aspects of talking to your son about sex is discussing what his peers have to say about it. This includes myths, slang terms and gossip. This vital information provides you with a better understanding of the information to which your son is exposed.

You can't wait for your son's father or your male friend to talk to him about sex. Many mothers opt to wait for the father or another significant male figure to talk about sex with their sons. While having another responsible man discuss sex with your son is important, you can't wait. With the Internet and exposure to MTV, VH1 and BET, boys are bombarded with images of sex. Thus, mothers can't afford to wait for the male perspective.

Additionally, we hope you will visit our Web site at www.raisinghimalone.com to participate in ongoing blog discussions about talking to your son about sex as well as other issues related to their development.

Raising Him Alone

Should He Get the Tattoo?

> Character is doing what's right when nobody's looking.
> **J. C. Watts, Jr.**

You have given your son everything he asked for, from the latest Trio cell phone to the new Jordan collection sneakers. Often you feel bad that his father has not "stepped up to the plate" so you're convinced that part of your responsibility is buying him the world.

Each year a new fad or trend captures your son's attention. Whether it's baggy jeans or a new electronic device, your son has convinced you to make the purchase no matter the cost. While you question each purchase; you eventually buckle under the pressure of making your son happy.

One Sunday afternoon after church Lisa Burroughs, a single mother raising a 14-year-old son in Oakland, Calif., is surprised by her son's request. As Lisa begins to explain, she prefaces her statement by letting us know her son is a good kid who's on the honor roll. You see, Lisa's son has requested a tattoo, and like many other young males, he's trying to convince his mother that the tattoo is safe and will symbolize his individuality.

For most parents the very thought of their son getting a tattoo creates a range of emotions from shock to anger. Tattoos have become part of a cultural landscape for young males. As early as elementary school, many boys begin using miscellaneous objects like pens, pencils, straight pins, ink, burnt metal objects, mascara and charcoal to make cheap tattoos. Furthermore, any examination of popular culture reveals that a large percentage of celebrity icons (Lil Wayne, Young Jeezy, Lebron James, Michael Jordan, Shawne Merriman, Tiger Woods, Shaquille O'Neal and Usher) have tattoos that appeal to young males. Tattoos have become fashionable and commonplace among young men in the NFL, NBA, Major Leagues and the music industry.

Like many issues confronting families, the issue of our sons wanting tattoos must be discussed. Your son wants to be cool and will be more concerned with his image than he should be. As a parent if you decide to let him get a tattoo, you must be concerned with the health-related aspects of doing so. Year in and year out, many unlicensed individuals are paid as little as $25 to put a tattoo on the arms of young men like your son. These illegal tattoos, created with dirty needles, can result in blood poisoning, skin disease, Hepatitis and even HIV. Following are a few suggested tips parents should consider about their sons' interest in getting a tattoo:

Parents should visit tattoo parlors with their sons and investigate them through the Better Business Bureau.

Parents must be willing to openly discuss their concerns about tattoos. Many unlicensed individuals who learned how to draw tattoos in prison operate in communities throughout this country. Parents should become familiar with state laws regarding tattoos. In many states minors under 18, even with parental consent, cannot get a tattoo in a reputable parlor.

Parents should understand tattoos can be removed at licensed centers that use lasers small enough for the body to flush out. The treatment can be very expensive. According to the American Academy of Facial Plastic and Reconstructive Surgery, it can run from $100 for a small, single-color tattoo with removal in one to two sessions to $500 per treatment to remove larger, multi-colored tattoos in as many as eight sessions (or as much as $4,000 depending on the size and color!)

Parents should discuss the long-term impact of tattoos. In today's society, many employers are reluctant about hiring young males with tattoos, particularly tattoos that are visible on the face and arms.

Parents who allow their minor sons to get tattoos should be clear on the meaning of the tattoos. Many young males get tattoos that promote gang affiliations and street terms like MOB (Money Over Bitches.) from $100 for a small, single-color tattoo with removal in one to two sessions to $500 per treatment to remove larger, multi-colored tattoos in as many as eight sessions (or as much as $4,000 depending on the size and color!)

Raising Him Alone

CHAPTER 5
Reconnecting Dads

I met him while working for a large bank in Houston. We were both college-educated and came from good homes. We discussed marriage and having a family. I can vividly remember the day I told him we were pregnant. Shortly after I gave birth he disappeared for several years. Our contact with each other was sporadic. Last August my son turned 4, and he unexpectedly showed up at the birthday party. I was angry but decided to put my hurt feelings aside to reconnect Jabar with his dad.

Single mother of one, Houston, Texas

FATHERLESS BOYS

This chapter is dedicated to beginning the discussion about reconnecting fathers. It is committed to redefining fathers as sober, responsible, spiritually guided men who are courageous enough to support their children and family unconditionally.

Regardless of obstacles and/or challenges which may arise, fatherhood requires an unyielding sense of commitment to ensure the safety and security of the family.

It doesn't take rocket science to see the effect absent fathers have on the emotional, physical and spiritual essence of Black male youth and young adults.

We believe fatherlessness is the most complex social issue confronting society. The issue of fatherlessness, while it impacts all families regardless of race, class and social economic status, is acute when we examine the Black community. Fatherlessness has created a "love deficit" within the Black community which has translated into alarming dropout rates, exploding incarceration rates and a generation of Black males under 18 who are willing to take the life of another person over money, jewelry and false notions of respect.

It is our hope that single mothers heed the call and

begin to think more seriously about parenting Black male children. With an alarming 70 percent of Black children and youth being raised by single mothers, the plight of our males rests solely on the shoulders of mothers.

This phenomenon must change if we are serious about raising healthy boys to become men. Within this process of reconnecting dads, mothers must be willing to move beyond the anger, hurt, pain and frustration to accept the reality that, if at all possible, boys need to have their fathers in their lives.

As Ray Davis, a social activist and dedicated father based in Baltimore shared with me, "Our sons need 8,760 hours of love from their fathers. This is equal to 365 days a year, 24 hours a day of support and guidance from a father."

BLAME GAME

So you had a baby by a man that you really didn't like. He was cute, a great dresser, drove a nice car and paid you more attention than any mother man. When you called him to tell him you were pregnant, his demeanor quickly changed. Six months into the pregnancy he decides he doesn't want any more children, making this revelation only after you guys had unprotected sex numerous times.

The day you go into labor you have your girlfriend call him on his cell phone while you are on your way to the hospital. Ten hours into labor you realize you are bringing a child into this world alone. The baby is born, and it is a beautiful, young Black male. While you are elated that you had a successful delivery, you are embarrassed to confide in your family and friends that you will be raising this boy alone.

Sound familiar? This story has become typical for too many Black mothers. Throughout the research on this book, this story was recounted numerous times by mothers across the country.

Often single mothers tend to blame themselves for the failed relationship. This blame manifests into poor relationship decisions, substance abuse, depression and anger issues.

One mother we interviewed in Columbus, Ga., told us she had become consumed with anger and jealousy. Her son's father remarried and was living in a gorgeous house about 20 miles away. The mother said she wished her son's father would have fallen on hard times after they separated.

Often, these feelings of anger stand in the way of single mothers supporting the healthy development of their sons.

TIPS FOR HELPING SINGLE MOTHERS COPE

Take some time to heal between relationships. Develop a healthy routine of activities that allows you to focus on lifestyle changes, including exercise and hobbies.

Focus on developing a game plan for your family – financial, educational, spiritual and personal. Always honor the decisions you have made, even if you think you made some mistakes along the way. Never make your son feel the burdens of your problems.

WHEN DAD WANTS TO COME BACK

Reconnecting absent dads can often become a challenging process for all parties involved. Many reasons may exist for the dad not being in his son's life. We find that absent dads fall in several different categories:

Come back dad – Dad is in and out of prison. He makes promises to his family that he can't honor. Provider – Dad doesn't see his son. His only interest is paying child support. He is often angry at his son's mother for many reasons. Usually he has multiple children by other women.

Broke Dad – He doesn't have a relationship with his son due to his resentment over an existing child support order. He works so much to pay for support that the last thing on his mind is developing an emotional relationship with his son.

While these categories do not represent all dads, we hope mothers and fathers will read this and begin having serious discussions about the role of a father. We realize reconnecting fathers with their sons can be a painful process. In many cases it has been years since father and son went to a ballgame, sat on a park bench and talked or simply went to the barbershop together.

Jennifer, a single mother of two energetic boys, shared with us that her sons' father was absent for several years. Jennifer never gave up hope. Each year she sent Christmas cards to her sons' father and signed their names to the card. Several days after Christmas 2006 he called saying he wanted to spend some time with his sons. Although Jennifer still struggles with the fact that he left, she has made a more concerted effort to involve her sons' father in their lives.

In many cases like Jennifer's, the healing process will be an ongoing journey that may require professional help from a licensed clinical social worker, psychologist or psychiatrist.

We believe rebuilding the family is the most logical way to ensure your son's success; however, we are in no way suggesting you and your son's father should start dating again.

QUICK TIPS FOR RECONNECTING FATHERS

Fathers may be absent for a number of reasons. These reasons may or may not be legitimate to you. However, it is important that fathers are allowed to be in their sons' lives.

> **1.** Realize it is critical for your son to have a relationship with his father, barring any previous issues of violence or unhealthy contact.
>
> **2.** Mom may need to initiate reconnecting and redefining the bond between the absent

father and her son. The male ego may not permit many fathers to extend the olive branch.

3. Mothers need to deal with their own issues related to improving the relationship between father and son.

4. If possible, have a one-on-one meeting with your son's father to discuss the parameters of the relationship.

5. Start slowly as this can be very emotional. Beginning by allowing your son to establish a telephone relationship with his father may be a great approach.

6. Create some one-on-one father and son opportunities.

7. Create an environment for open communication between your son and his father.

8. Create opportunities for the three of you to openly talk about the relationship.

HE CAN NEVER BE THE MAN OF YOUR HOUSE

Do you know any mother who refers to her son as "little man" or "the man of the house?" If so, strongly recommend that she ceases this practice immediately because of the mixed messages it can send the male child. Please note, mom, even if your son is paying the cable bill, he is not the man of the house and shouldn't be labeled as such.

In a keynote address given at the Young Men Employment Network Student Conference in Kean University in 2006, noted scholar and historian Dr. Lenworth Gunther outlined how Hip hop music sends the message to young people that it is cool and consequently acceptable to remain "little." He points to a number of rappers but insists this phenomenon did not start with Hip hop. During the 1950s and 1960s, there were a few people who referred to themselves as "little," including Little Richard and Little Anthony of Little Anthony and the Imperials. Recently, however, this trend has grown and now a greater number of entertainers have adopted little – or the notion of remaining young – as part of their persona: Little John, Lil Wayne, Little Scrappy, Little Kim, Little Cee, the former Little Bow Wow (now Bow Wow) and Destiny's Child – if your destiny is to be a child you will never grow up. All of these young people are at least 21; some are parents and they all are millionaires.

While I see the financial incentives for entertainers to refer to themselves as "little," there is no such incentive for young men in general to do so. Their mothers should not refer to them as little anything, especially not "little man."

| *Raising Him Alone*

This concept is an oxymoron like "jumbo shrimp," and it has the potential to send the incorrect message to boys that there is such a thing as a "little man." The term "little" generally refers to something that is small or less than, whereas the term man is generally associated with being a provider and protector. Therefore, the term "little man" makes absolutely no sense, should not be considered cute and at all costs should be eliminated due to its potential of preventing a male child from recognizing his destiny of becoming a man, husband and father. After all, should children refer to their father as "Little Daddy?" Likewise, should wives refer to their spouses as "Little Husbands?" No!

Lastly, a word on the use of the phrase "Man of The House." We believe the only way a son can be the man of the house in which his mother lives is if he is paying all of the bills. This can be the case if the mother is mandated to move into his house or he is required to take over her financial responsibilities due to an illness or old age. Otherwise, he can't possibly take on this role because he is not able to respond to the expectations. Under normal circumstances the man of the house is usually responsible for three main tasks: honoring God by guiding his family spiritually, providing financial stability and protecting his family in all aspects. The other side of this coin is the privilege of being the man of the house, which a mother could never fulfill. Besides getting the biggest piece of chicken at the dinner table, the man of the house should not expect a level of honor and respect that his mother can not or should not exhibit.

At some point you may have to cut the "apron strings." Having your son move out is a normal part of the life cycle.

The following are a few helpful tips:
Begin the discussion about "life after high school" early. Develop an understanding of what your son is good at. Realize that college is not for everyone and explore trade schools and other options.
Begin visiting career fairs in his freshman year.

Village Dad

A good friend and mentor, Adeyemi Bandele, often speaks affectionately about the Village Dad. For many generations of African-American families the notion of growing up in a community was commonplace. When I talk about community I am referring to people living in a targeted area who share common values, parenting rituals and community development practices.

In a community it was not rare for the majority of stakeholders to have relationships and participate in functions like informal community cleanups and community cookouts.

Growing up, boys naturally respected and had meaningful relationships with older men in the community. These were men you would see in the barbershop, cutting grass and on their way to church on Sunday. To a boy, many of these men were larger than life.

We didn't realize it at the time, but these men were "Village Dads." Boys growing up in the community had a physical and emotional connection to these men. Growing up, boys realized that these men had the ability to correct them when they were wrong and, equally important, to praise them for good deeds.

Although so many of these men had been involved in drug dealing and other criminal activities, they respected the community.

Absent of biological fathers, all boys need to have access to "Village Dads." This may be difficult in many communities due to the challenges that men face; however, we still believe that many men are able to serve as "Village Dads."

The following are just a few things "Village Dads" provide:

> An opportunity for boys to understand manhood and masculinity.

> Helping boys understand their limits and boundaries. When boys are around real men they understand and exercise their limits. Often, things they do around their mothers they will not do around a collective of men.

An acceptance of male codes, or high levels of energy that promote physical interaction – wrestling, jumping, tumbling and other opportunities to release energy.

Teaching boys a language which accepts and honors their pride and helps them understand their emotions.

| *Raising Him Alone*

CHAPTER 6
Amazing Grandparents

I have raised my own children and now I am raising my children's children. Drugs nearly devastated my family. As a result of the ill of crack cocaine, I have adopted my two grandsons.

Single grandmother of two boys, New Haven, CT.

Grandparents Raising Boys: The New Generation of Amazing Grandparents

Lisa Reagan, a 64-year-old grandmother living in Birmingham, AL., retired after 32 years in the healthcare industry. Recently Ms. Reagan applied for a part-time job at a local convenience store to make ends meet. She is a grandmother caring for three young boys ages 7, 9 and 11. Ms. Reagan represents a growing group of grandparents who are now raising a generation of young Black males. She joins the ranks of "Amazing grandmother!" Raising boys at any age can be difficult, but when Ms. Reagan was 64 her daughter started using drugs and became unable to care for her sons. Ms. Reagan fought for custody and won. It is difficult and some days, Ms. Reagan admits, "Raising a boy in today's society is hard. When I raised my son, gangs were not an issue and schools seemed like they cared about children. Now it seems that many schools have given up on young Black males."

Grandparents raising another generation of children may seem like an abnormal situation, but across the country it has become the norm. Whether it's due to death, mental illness, incarceration, drugs, alcoholism and/or parental neglect, record numbers of children are forced to live with their grandparents. According to the 2000 census, there were 6 million children living with their grandparents, a 30 percent increase from 1990.

Often these grandmothers struggle to cope with the daily challenges associated with raising young children, including checking homework, preparing meals and enforcing discipline, which can be overwhelming.

Additionally, a large percentage of these grandmothers have their own health challenges, including high blood pressure and diabetes. All too often these grandparents struggle financially to make ends meet and provide for the new additions to their family.

Finally, the Raising Him Alone campaign is committed to supporting amazing grandparents raising male children. Please visit the Raising Him Alone Web site at www.raisinghimalone.com for additional parenting strategies.

Here are some tips on raising your grandson and creating a balanced, healthy lifestyle:

Maintain family relationships. Develop family traditions and rituals to maintain family connections. Even if the parents are locked up, it's important to maintain some form of communication. In a case of incarceration, letters can be an effective means of communicating. If transportation is available and you are up to it, consider taking your grandson to prison – depending on his age and maturity/emotional levels – for an occasional visit.

Get involved in your grandson's school. Grandparents should make sure they visit the school and attend school-related activities.

Advocate for your grandchild. For whatever reason, you are raising your grandson. He lives with you and you are responsible for his health and well being. It is important that you become involved in all aspects of your grandson's life.

Open lines of communication. Raising male grandchildren can be difficult because of the generation between grandparents and grandchildren. Grandparents need to be receptive to understanding different lifestyles and trends. Being able to communicate with your grandson about music, video games, dating and other things that represent his world is important.

Honesty is key. Depending on the age of your grandson, being honest about the situation of his parents is important. Obviously, you don't want to tell a 4-year-old that his parents are drug addicts, but an 11-year-old likely could handle being told.

Be consistent about family rules. Boys need structure. Grandparents must set clear rules and stick to them. Often grandparents over compensate for the loss of parents and use gifts as ways to maintain the relationship with their grandsons. It is not a good idea and, frankly, it's a hard pattern to break once begun.

FINAL THOUGHTS FOR GRANDPARENTS

Check list
A few things for grandparents to consider when raising boys

- ☐ Boys need unconditional love, even during the times you don't really like them.

- ☐ Boys need rules and should be taught they must follow the rules or suffer the consequences.

- ☐ Boys need attention but shouldn't be the center of it at all times.

- ☐ Boys must have responsibilities in order to become responsible.

- ☐ Boys must know the theory of give and take.

- ☐ Boys must be taught how to give and receive love.

- ☐ Boys must learn that respect for others is so important, and so is self respect.

- ☐ Remember, caring for and about others helps boys become well-rounded.

- ☐ And please remember that a good, balanced education is absolutely vital in today's world for boys to become successful.

CHAPTER 7
Final Thoughts

Can you image what our communities would look like if 100% of our sons had a meaningful relationship with their father?

Raising Him Alone was written to support the positive development of male youth. As you read the book you will find a singular theme that permeates the book. "Our sons are worth saving." This theme resonates among the hundreds of single mothers and grandmothers that we interviewed for background information for the book and to launch the Raising Him Alone Campaign.

We feel strongly that supporting single mothers and grandmothers during their journey to parent male children can make a dramatic impact on the socialization of boys. Daily we are bombarded with negative images and stereotypes about Black families and Black males. It has been a labor of love meeting so many single mothers from across the U.S. and abroad who are high intelligent, hard working and excellent parents. Many mothers that we interview defy many of the myths associated with single parents. Several mothers that we interviewed had law degrees and Ph.d's from some of the most exclusive colleges and universities throughout country. At the end of the day single mothers are just like other mothers who want the best for their sons.

Raising Him Alone

Each chapter in the book focused on specific areas that mothers and grandmothers indicated as topics and or subjects which caused them a great deal of anxiety. Whether dealing with talking to your son about sex to discussing the pros and cons of your teenage son getting a tattoo Raising Him Alone provides concrete recommendations to support positive parenting strategies.

While we realize that no one book can answer every questions about single mothers raising a boy we believe that Raising Him Alone begins an important community discussion around the challenges and successes of single mothers raising boys.

Additionally, the following are just a few things that we hope single mothers and grandmothers will think about:

1. Teaching your son the importance of integrity

2. Developing a new found respect for girls and women

3. Mothers play a major role in helping sons learn value lessons about love, empathy and compassion

4. Importance of connecting your son to sober, responsible & spiritually guided men

5. Join a support group for single mothers and grandmothers (if one doesn't exist start one)

Raising Him Alone

Finally, after reading Raising Him Alone we hope that you will begin to think more critically about your role as a "guiding" force in the life of your son.

ABOUT THE AUTHORS

David Miller, M.Ed.

David C. Miller, M.Ed., is Co-founder and Chief Visionary Officer of the Urban Leadership Institute, LLC, (www.urbanyouth.org)a social enterprise that focuses on creating positive youth development strategies. ULI provides strategic planning, professional development, positive youth development concepts and crisis management services.

A former middle school educator in a tough Baltimore school district, Miller incorporates his keen insight into youth trends, community dynamics and empowerment strategies designed to motivate youth and adults from diverse backgrounds.

Miller is the architect of the Dare to Be King Project (www.daretobeking.com), a community based intervention that addresses anger, decision making and moral reasoning among African-American males 12 to 17. The project features seminars, workshops and a comprehensive curriculum designed to empower African-American males as well as motivate and inspire the professionals who work with them. The Dare to Be King Project uses a Rites of Passage framework to address many of the complex, social issues that confront African-American males in society by providing practical alternatives to community violence, substance abuse, delinquency, etc.

Miller is the author of several books, including **Dare to Be King: What If The Prince Lives?** a Survival Workbook for African-American Males (2003, 2004 & 2008), **Lessons I Learned from My Father: A Collection of Quotes from Men of African Descent** (2004), **Dare to Be Queen: Wholistic Curriculum for Working with Girls** (2005) **Rhyme & Reason a Hip Hop Curriculum for Professionals who Work wit Teens** (2005) and **Daddy's Girl: Remembering Advice From My Father** (2006). Miller is currently working on **Educating the Educators: Lessons Learned from Public School Teachers** (September 2010).

Miller is a graduate of Goucher College (Master's in Education) and the University of Baltimore (B.S. in Political Science).

Matt Stevens

Matthew P. Stevens is Founder of Empower Today's Youth LLC, which provides youth who are at least 13-years-old with at-risk tools including critical thinking and decision making that are necessary for healthy life decisions.

Stevens, an author, presenter, youth counselor and freshman college advisor, has had a lifelong passion for empowering today's youth.

His comprehensive Youth Empowerment Program provides a Behavioral Modification Curriculum for parents, teachers, counselors and administrators in the public and private sectors to support the needs of at-risk youth. Stevens is a graduate of Bloomfield College and Certificate in Mentor Supervision from Fordham University.

notes